# THE LAST CATHEDRAL

(Photo by Hal Siegel)

# THE LAST CATHEDRAL

## TY HARRINGTON

PRENTICE-HALL, INC., Englewood Cliffs, New Jersey

Book Designer, Linda Huber
Art Director, Hal Siegel

All photographs courtesy Ty Harrington,
unless otherwise noted.

Printed in the United States of America
Prentice-Hall International, Inc., London
Prentice-Hall of Australia, Pty. Ltd., Sydney
Prentice-Hall of Canada, Ltd., Toronto
Prentice-Hall of India Private Ltd., New Delhi
Prentice-Hall of Japan, Inc., Tokyo
Prentice-Hall of Southeast Asia Pte. Ltd., Singapore
Whitehall Books Limited, Wellington, New Zealand
10 9 8 7 6 5 4 3 2 1

**Library of Congress Cataloging in Publication Data**
Harrington, Ty.
The last cathedral.
1. Washington, D. C. Cathedral of St. Peter and
St. Paul. I. Title.
NA5235.W3H37     726'.6'09753     79-11976
ISBN 0-13-523878-1

 TO MY FATHER

The author gratefully acknowledges the help of Harvey Arden, Wolf Von Eckardt, Clerk of the Works Richard Feller, Canon Michael Hamilton, Dale Hushbeck, Kenneth Lynch, Nancy S. Montgomery, Sally Pearse Morris, Patrick Munroe, Nancy Perry, Dean Francis B. Sayre, Barbara L. Scott, Claudia Velletri, Nancy Watson, Julie Wilson, and Harvey Yellin.

# CONTENTS

# INTRODUCTION

It was a quiet Sunday morning, April-perfect weather for an early constitutional along the Chesapeake and Ohio canal below Georgetown. As I walked across Key Bridge from Virginia, the monumental white buildings before me stood silhouetted against the cobalt sky; never since I moved to Washington had it looked so much like a capital city. I began listening to the distant sound of bells, counting the peals in the hope they would tell the time. But it was not the quarter-hour ring of my college chapel. These bells rang on and on. When an occasional beat was missed I realized the bells were being rung by hand. And by counting the notes I guessed there were about seven bells. (In fact, there were ten.)

Now a single bell with a pull rope is quite common in many churches, if only as a manual auxiliary to recorded chimes piped out through loudspeakers. Real change ringing, however, is rare—especially on this side of the Atlantic, where the number of such bells and the "bands" that play them can almost be counted on the fingers of one hand.

Never having heard peal bells in Washington, I began to look about for a bell tower. And there it was, tall and stately, unmistakably Gothic, against the cloudless sky. Foregoing my stroll, I went back for my car and drove toward the landmark suddenly visible from miles away. I had discovered the National Cathedral!

The National Cathedral is an overwhelming architectural concept even in these hyperbolic days. Situated atop Mount St. Alban, the District of Columbia's highest point, the Cathedral overlooks the Washington Monument by nearly one hundred feet, and provides the grandest view of the city to be found. Spanning a tenth of a mile, it is the fifth largest cathedral in the world, thirty yards longer than Notre Dame, and covering twice the area of Salisbury. Its Gothic shadows stretch across a meticulously groomed fifty-seven-acre close, which includes two private schools and a college where students prepare lessons in a timeless atmosphere of beauty and serenity.

Every aspect of the Cathedral inspires awe and admiration for the munificence of its treasures, the product of several generations and many hundreds of craftsmen laboring for almost eighty years. Stoneworkers, often working with tools invented long before the Middle Ages, have raised arches and walls and towers, and have set in place building blocks weighing several tons apiece with incredible precision. Sculptors and carvers have given the stone character, chiseling scores of gargoyles, hundreds of angels, and thousands of crockets and finials. Inside, jeweled color illuminates the aisles and transepts, the nave and choir with a continuously changing light show from the stained-glass windows. (One rose window alone contains more than 255 colors and shades.) In short,

(Photo by Hal Siegel)

the National Cathedral is a unique structure—a magnificent gift to the nation wholly funded by thousands of private donors. Open to all people, it is a fitting legacy, a final statement, a memorial to knowledge and skills that have almost ceased to exist and may soon be lost to the ages.

The great tragedy of the glorious medieval cathedrals is that their creators have been largely anonymous. The National Cathedral, probably the last great Gothic cathedral that will ever be built, provides a final opportunity to delve into the individual relationships of the craftsmen with their work. In this book I have tried to provide a glimpse into the minds and hearts of this unique breed of men. I learned what I could about them, from mason and muralist, architect and ironworker, before they too pass into history.

In some crafts only a few artisans still exist, and they are not being replaced. In 1946, for example, the American Stone Cutters and Carvers Guild numbered more than one hundred and fifty carvers in New York City alone. Today there are fewer than one hundred stone carvers in the entire country.

In addition, the cost of building a Gothic cathedral, with all its special requirements, is becoming increasingly prohibitive. Building a Gothic cathedral in twentieth-century America is a far cry from building one in fourteenth-century Europe, especially when it receives no financial support from church or state. In 1978 a shortage of funds brought construction to a halt for the fourth time. While this is almost traditional for Gothic cathedrals, today there is an important difference: if there are too many delays, craftsmen with these skills and of this caliber may no longer be available, and without them, the Cathedral as originally envisioned can never be completed.

Despite the narrowing odds, however, the Building Committee and the workers who remain are as adamant as the enduring stone in which they work; somehow, they say, they will see the task to completion. Nevertheless, as Master Carver Roger Morigi said to me shortly before his seventieth birthday, "In the world of today, patience is gone and there is no more desire to build things that last. Times have changed and cathedrals are too hard work. The young craftsmen are too few, the costs are too high. There will never be another building like this—this is the last cathedral."

*Washington, D.C.*

*Looking down from the roof walk.*

# BUILDING THE
# NATIONAL CATHEDRAL

*Mankind was never so happily inspired as when it made a cathedral:*
*a thing as single and as spacious as a statue to the first glance,*
*and yet, on examination, as lively and interesting as a forest in detail.*
*The height of the spires cannot be taken by trigonometry; they measure*
*absurdly short, but how tall they are to the admiring eye. . . .*
Robert Louis Stevenson

In 1791 Pierre L'Enfant, a French engineer and soldier who had fought for the Colonies under Lafayette, was commissioned by President Washington to lay out plans for a "capital city" to be built at the confluence of the Anacostia and Potomac rivers. In his design for the District of Columbia, L'Enfant, at Washington's request, included a site for a "church for national purposes to serve as a moral lighthouse for the nation, a house of prayer for all Americans." The Constitution, however, firm in its separation of church and state, made it impossible to expend federal funds for the building of even a "national" church.

The new world capital grew slowly. Column by column, one massive structure after another was erected. In 1891, as L'Enfant's plan was being completed, the subject of a national church was once again raised. A group of twenty-one Episcopalians had banded together to generate interest in a free church "open to all people . . . shared with all people . . . maintained only by people who give as they are able," a church to be financed not by a single congregation, but by people of every faith and creed joining together in a common cause, funded by private donations alone.

In 1893 President Benjamin Harrison indicated his support for the project by signing a Congressional Charter empowering the Protestant Episcopal Cathedral Foundation "to establish and maintain within the District of Columbia a cathedral and institutions of learning for the promotion of religion and education and charity." Some eighty-five years later, the Cathedral is a reality, built slowly and patiently, stone by stone, one

piece of glass at a time–a labor of love in every detail of its creation. Though it has been a costly project, it has remained true to its original purpose, and no funds from industry, organized church, or government have been used since the foundation stone was set in 1907.

Gradually the Cathedral has assumed its role as a truly national church.* Its deans and bishops have been consulted by national leaders on issues of morality. Scheduled events, such as Leonard Bernstein's performance of Haydn's Mass in Time of War, during the crisis of 1973, have encouraged those with differing points of view to use the Cathedral as a neutral meeting place. It has been chosen for state funerals and official eulogies. Over the years the National Cathedral has served as home to churchless congregations, and within its walls services have been conducted for the members of many faiths. It has no congregation of its own but is always open to all Americans.

The Gothic cathedral is a blossoming in stone subdued by the insatiable demand of harmony in man.
Ralph Waldo Emerson

With charter in hand, those who were to become the Cathedral's first Building Committee began soliciting funds with which to purchase a site. The first gift was from a schoolteacher who gave forty dollars, saved from the sale of her needlework, "for a free

---

*Note on nomenclature. Though it is officially named the Cathedral Church of St. Peter and St. Paul, the Cathedral is more often referred to as the Washington Cathedral or the National Cathedral. In keeping with its founders' intention to create "a great church for national purposes," I have chosen to refer to it throughout the book as the National Cathedral.

*The Reverend Avery Dulles, S.J., speaks from the Canterbury pulpit.* (Photo by Morton Broffman)

church on Alban Hill." Donations soon began to arrive from every state. After several years of searching, and considering various sites in turn, land was purchased (as the teacher had requested) on top of Mount St. Alban, Washington's highest point.

In 1901 plans were drawn for the fifty-seven-acre Cathedral close, and the Committee proceeded to discuss the style of architecture the buildings should follow. All "contemporary" styles were promptly eliminated because of the likelihood they would soon appear dated. At first the Committee was inclined toward Classic Revival, the architecture employed for most of Washington's government buildings. These magnificent structures, reminiscent of ancient Greece, provided elegant office space for the extensive system of federal bureaus and, they felt, gave an air of dignity and stability to the city.

When the Building Committee went on to explore the possibilities of other styles, however, Gothic stood out as particularly suited to the religious statement they had always envisioned–an expression of faith in the unity of mankind. No other style, they noted, "...permits so much versatility in the design of both the interior and the exterior." Moreover, they reasoned, Gothic architecture was developed specifically to express man's relationship to his surroundings and his origin. As John Ruskin (1819–1900, English art critic and essayist) once wrote, "Gather a branch from any of the trees or flowers to which the earth owes its principal beauty and you will find every one of its leaves is terminated, more or less, in the form of a pointed arch; and it is to that form that [Gothic architecture] owes its grace and character."

Gothic architecture begins with a cat's cradle of arches. The interior projects a feeling of having been created by something greater than man, with slender supporting piers that carry the vaulting to fantastic heights. The exterior draws you closer to explore the never-ending detail. If architecture is the most collective of all arts, then

*Sculpture and shadow pattern the balcony of the north porch.*

Gothic architecture is the most collective of all architectural styles.

"In one point of view," wrote Ruskin in his *Stones of Venice*, "Gothic is not only the best, but the most rational, architecture, as being that which can fit itself most easily into all services...." Although Gothic employs many architectural forms that were developed prior to the twelfth century, Gothic builders were the first to combine these diverse elements into a single style of expression. The result was a wholly new concept of architecture: a constant fusion of the plastic with the monumental, with greater structural potential than had ever been possible before. Never until then had man been able to build so high, yet so gracefully, with such enormous windows filling every wall. In addition, with the development of the Gothic style, architecture became only one of the ingredients in a "classical" coming together of the arts.

The development of the Gothic form was an architectural leap forward. And it came at a time when mankind had a greater passion for the collective task of building than ever before in the Western world. Between 1170 and 1270, eighty great cathedrals and nearly five hundred churches of cathedral size were built in France alone–among them some of the finest structures ever raised by man. During the Middle Ages there was a church for every two hundred people, and as these mostly Romanesque buildings were one by one destroyed by fire they were replaced mainly with Gothic masonry, much of which still stands today. Not only did the Gothic cathedral bring together a diversity of crafts, but a single cathedral was often the product of an entire community working together for several generations to complete it. And while Romanesque abbeys had been built in earlier times primarily to serve as monasteries, the new cathedrals were designed to address the needs of growing cities in a burgeoning Europe, and the immense area of the nave was meant to accommodate a town's whole population during festivals and holidays.

The return of the Crusaders, who brought back a different culture from the Middle East, spurred the birth of Gothic architecture. In this sense, Gothic was more than merely an architectural style; it represented changing times as well as a change in medieval man's view of himself. Its development was accompanied by a rebirth of the study of geometry, astronomy, and natural laws. There was a renewed search for truth by means of rational thought, and from this new metaphysics a kind of "Gothic thought" emerged, an intellectual approach to measure and mass. Architects of the time were expected to be both mathematicians and artists, and were respected as among the most learned of men. The culmination of this change came with Abbot Suger's rebuilding of the St.-Denis Cathedral.

In 1134 Abbot Suger was in the process of renovating the Abbey Church of St.-Denis, just outside of Paris. Suger had political ambitions, and he sought to build a structure that would win him a position of influence. In drawing the plans for St.-Denis, he departed from the traditional rounded Norman arch, and used instead a pointed vaulting with a single keystone as its center of pressure. The use of the pointed arch revolutionized the design of the ribbing, allowing it to be linked together as never before; a taller, narrower structure was now possible. Suger developed his new techniques with contemporary concepts of geometry, and he wove an intricate skeleton of mathematically precise proportions. The result had a visual impact far greater than might have been expected from an examination of the parts. "Harmony," Suger wrote, "is the source of all beauty, since it exemplifies the laws according to which divine reason has constructed the universe." It was Suger who originated what has since become the central theme of all Gothic designs–a control of light and line based upon the foliage of the forest, the "natural" order that is found in the randomly structured "harmony of the woods."

The invention of the buttress, and especially the flying buttress–first used in the building of the Cathedral of Notre Dame in Paris–added stability by transferring stress away from the walls. By means of complex mathematical computations, the need for stress-bearing walls was eliminated; now windows could be built where previously solid masonry was necessary to support the roof. As Ruskin noted, "No segment of interior space was allowed to remain in the dark, undefined by light."

Suger completed St.-Denis in 1144, and by 1170 Gothic cathedrals were being built all across France. Their embellishments served as a Bible for the illiterate, telling in paintings, mosaics, and stained glass the stories most people were unable to read, and the exteriors–facing as they usually did onto the marketplace–were decorated so as to attract the attention of passersby and draw them into church. Lines of masonry, static in previous styles, were now arranged to give a feeling of movement, luring onlookers toward the portals, capturing them with an uplifting sense of awe. Only a century after St.-Denis was finished, Gothic had spread far and wide, and had become the most influential style in the history of architecture, employing in the process a good part of the population.

> In Gothic times writing, painting, carving, casting, it mattered not what–were all works done by thoughtful happy men; and the illumination of the volume and the carving and casting of wall and gate, employed not thousands, but millions of true and noble artists all over Christian lands.
>
> John Ruskin

*The south transept and the Gloria in Excelsis Tower.*

On May 21, 1906, after nearly five years of research into various architectural possibilities, the Building Committee of the National Cathedral decided that the new Cathedral would be in the style that began with St.-Denis. "Gothic was chosen," explained Francis Sayre, dean of the Cathedral for twenty-five years until his retirement in 1978, "because it is symbolic, unlike modern life which bombards you with hundreds of millions of words through every medium.

Gothic invites you to see with your eyes, your ears, using all of your senses to hunt out a meaning."

Even back in 1906 the Building Committee members were aware of the direction the twentieth century was taking. Values had already deteriorated, and the world placed emphasis more on quantity than on quality. The assembly line and other devices of mass production were firmly entrenched; precision craftsmanship was on the wane, and individuals were increasingly reluctant to plan projects that might extend beyond their own lifetimes. Even as the committee elected the

Gothic style, they wondered whether there would be artists and craftsmen, draftsmen and fabricators who would understand and could accept the demanding Gothic concept of perfection in every detail. Would they have enough of the patience, born of a passion for their work, that is required if a craftsman is to devote his skills to the painstaking embellishment of a cathedral?

With the style chosen, the Building Committee began to search for an architect capable of an authentic Gothic design. The Committee initially leaned toward opening up the selection process by announcing the building of the Cathedral publicly, and by encouraging all interested architects to submit their ideas for consideration. It was hoped that this "competition" would draw a response from yet-unknown architects as well as from those who already had a reputation. But the Committee soon realized there was a fundamental weakness in the idea of open selection. Even the most excellently drafted plans would not necessarily indicate that the designer had a practical, working knowledge of Gothic construction. After all, Gothic masonry alone was a technically demanding, highly specialized craft requiring on-the-site experience, and the architect they chose had to know not only masonry, but many, many other elements of Gothic construction. The Building Committee concluded that it would be useless for them to review architects' plans without first receiving some sort of assurance the plans could be realized. At this juncture, the Committee and Bishop of Washington Henry Yates Satterlee decided to seek out only those men who had had actual experience in Gothic construction, and to choose from among them the Cathedral's first architect.

Although many Americans had studied Gothic architecture, none had had sufficient practical experience to supervise a structure with the enormous scope of a cathedral. In September 1906 Bishop Satterlee sailed for

*A profile view of a corner of the south transept at the clerestory level.*

England. The British Isles had for generations been a center for specialized Gothic study. Many British architects were well versed in Gothic construction, as they had been constantly called upon to assist in the maintenance of the many great medieval structures on both sides of the English Channel. The Archbishop of Canterbury and others whom Bishop Satterlee consulted suggested that he consider George Frederick Bodley, as he was the architect with perhaps the greatest insight into Gothic design and

8

construction. Bodley, then seventy-nine years of age, had served as partner architect to Giles Gilbert Scott in designing Liverpool Cathedral. He had also designed the Beaux Arts School in Paris and many other Gothic structures throughout the world. In 1889 he had been awarded the gold medal of the Royal Institute of British Architects for his work on Gothic churches.

Bishop Satterlee was so impressed with Bodley's ideas that he invited the architect to accompany him back to Washington. Bodley did so and when he saw the Mount St. Alban site expressed his enthusiasm. He agreed to stay in Washington and that same fall made some rough sketches for the Building Committee. The Committee, encouraged by Bodley's suggestions, asked if he would be willing to work up a set of preliminary plans. Bodley agreed and returned to England to draw the detailed drafts. Pleased though they were with Bodley, the Building Committee was nevertheless concerned because there was no American architect involved. They felt that "only an American could understand American conditions, American life, and American workmen." To solve this problem the Committee sent a cable to Bodley asking if he would be willing to work in collaboration with an American architect. Bodley swiftly replied, "Willing to be partner to good American architect," and suggested Boston's Henry Vaughan.

After considering several other possibilities, the Building Committee did ask Vaughan to join Bodley. Vaughan was ideally suited to the partnership. Born in 1845, he had studied in England under Bodley before starting his own practice in Boston. He had won acclaim for his design of St. Paul's Chapel, and for the chapel he built for Groton School in Connecticut.

Working together again, Bodley and Vaughan completed the preliminary drawings for the Cathedral. On June 10, 1907, their plans were accepted by the Building Commit-

tee and they were formally named Cathedral architects. On September 29 of that same year President Theodore Roosevelt struck the last blow on the Cathedral's foundation stone, using the same mason's gavel George Washington had used to set the cornerstone for the U.S. Capitol in 1793. Just two weeks after this auspicious start, George Bodley died, and Vaughan was left to carry the plans forward alone.

Vaughan made modifications in the original design almost immediately, making provisions for a crypt chapel at Bishop Satterlee's request. Construction began late in 1909, and by 1912 the first service was held in Bethlehem Chapel, as it was called, located beneath what was to become the Cathedral's apse. By 1915 Vaughan had completed working plans for the apse and the choir, and building of the superstructure was started. In 1917, however, with the first sections almost completed, Henry Vaughan died suddenly at the age of seventy-two, leaving the Cathedral without an architect. The Building Committee began their search anew; but now they had to find not only a capable Gothic architect but one who was also able and willing to take up where Bodley and Vaughan had left off, without detracting from their design.

The Committee's problems were solved unexpectedly when they received an unsolicited paper prepared by an accomplished, but relatively unknown, architect named Philip Hubert Frohman. Frohman had visited the Cathedral as a tourist in 1912 and had been so taken with it that he had written beside his signature in Bethlehem Chapel's visitors' book that he dreamed of someday becoming the Cathedral architect. Five years later, when Frohman heard of Vaughan's death, he put together some of his thoughts about the design of the Cathedral and sent them to the Building Committee.

The Committee was greatly impressed with Frohman's proposals and asked him to submit more detailed sketches, showing how

*Original design of the west facade by Donald Robb—revised by Philip Frohman.*

*Architect's rendering of the West Front, April 1959.*

he would proceed with the development of Bodley and Vaughan's preliminary plans. Frohman asked Donald Robb, an architect noted for his draftsmanship and sketch work of Gothic designs, to assist him; Robb agreed and they went to work. A year later Frohman and Robb were joined in their partnership by Harry B. Little, one of the architects who designed the Cathedral of St. John the Divine in New York City.

In November of 1921, after two years of revising and augmenting Bodley's original plans for the crypt, to which Frohman added the Norman ambulatories and the Chapel of the Resurrection, Frohman, Robb, and Little were officially appointed architects to the Cathedral. From then until their deaths in the early 1940s, both Robb and Little assisted continually in drafting the plans. Robb's skills are especially apparent in his drawings for the keystone bosses in the choir and the sanctuary; his sketches are so detailed that carvers were able to convert many of them directly into stone without the usual plaster models. Among Little's many contributions, the vaulting for the Children's Chapel is considered his finest.

It was Frohman, however, who served as the Cathedral's principal designer, and he assumed as well the responsibility of supervising its construction. Toward the end of 1919, he had moved to Washington so that he could devote his full attention to the Cathedral; Robb and Little retained their headquarters in Boston. In all, Frohman served as Cathedral architect for more than fifty years, and is recognized as the one person most responsible for the architectural character of the National Cathedral as it exists today–a cathedral that is considered the finest Gothic structure of modern times.

Building an original Gothic cathedral in the twentieth century is an unusual task. But Philip Hubert Frohman was a most unusual man–no one ever doubted he was a genius. However, because of the medieval values he placed on time and quality, values that did

*The apse, circa 1919.*

Throop Polytechnic Institute in Pasadena, California. He later wrote: "During that year our English class was treated to a very good illustrated lecture on Westminster Abbey. It was that which caused me to become more seriously interested in cathedrals, so that eventually church architecture became the objective of my continuing interest in the sciences and the arts."

Frohman was fourteen years old when he designed his first building, which still stands today. Going on from Throop to study architecture at the California Institute of Technology, he opened his first office at the age of twenty-one and was named Cathedral Architect only ten years later. From then on, until he was seventy, Frohman was up in the scaffolding every single day, often climbing several stories by ladder to examine work in progress. Master Mason Billy Cleland remembers that even when Frohman was in his eighties he was still actively involved in the construction, often climbing the scaffolding several times a week.

Frohman was a quietly enthusiastic man, possessed of great personal reserve. During more than fifty years of working with the Cathedral staff he never called anyone by his first name, preferring to address him as "Mister." Soft-spoken and diffident in manner, he was also gently in control of every situation. He once explained it was part of his philosophy of life. "The mind should control the body and the mind should be directed by the spirit." He went on, quoting a verse he had learned as a child, "For greater is he who ruleth his spirit than he who taketh a city."

In 1972, after being hit by a truck as he walked down the North Drive of the Cathedral's close, Frohman died at the age of eighty-five.

His entire life was dedicated to building the Cathedral, but because of his insistence on perfection, as if time were limitless, Frohman would probably never have completed the plans for the west facade without the constant urging of Richard Feller, who had

not coincide with the ever-increasing pace of this century, he was sometimes regarded as an anachronism. To this charge he replied, "I would not object to being called an anachronism ... provided the term could also apply to a person who is not concerned with the past alone, but who can also place himself at a time in the future and from that position look back upon both the past and the present, and govern his actions accordingly."

Philip Hubert Frohman was born in 1887, the son of Gustave Frohman, brother of the well-known theatrical producers Charles and Daniel Frohman. At an early age Philip decided he wanted to make architecture his life's work. When he turned eleven, he persuaded his parents to enroll him in the been appointed Clerk of the Works in 1957. According to Jack Fanfani, Feller's assistant and right hand, "Dick Feller had his hands full convincing Frohman to finish the plans to the point where someone else could take over and build his designs. The problem wasn't that he was getting old, it was just that he had no respect for time. He was not driven in that sense of the word. Feller had to convince him to leave some of the details until he was done with the overall plans. Frohman was always concerned with completing one project exactly before he would go on to the next. Careful, methodical, and thoroughly interested in each problem as it arose, solving one at a time. And if he determined that a tracery molding should be cut at four and three-eighths inches, instead of the four and five-sixteenths he had indicated, he wouldn't hesitate to change a whole set of drawings."

G. Gardner Monks of the Building Committee wrote about Frohman in much the same vein: "He is insistent almost to a point that drives one to distraction that the design should be as nearly perfect as he is able to make it. Hours spent on blueprints to change the radius of an arch by an inch seem to mean nothing to him if he is convinced that thereby the building would be improved.... Mr. Frohman is meticulous. Needless to say, he is painstaking in attention to detail. It becomes almost an article of religious faith with him that there should be no shoddy or slip-shod designing or construction allowed to make its way into the Cathedral. For a person who is admittedly a genius I find him extraordinarily amenable to suggestions, many of which will prove to be beside the point, and he is extraordinarily easy to talk to.... He has a genuine humility of spirit that is quite rare in a person of his unquestioned artistic genius."

Frohman was intimately concerned with everything that involved any aspect of the building, including the embellishing and furnishing of the Cathedral. The central files are full of details of his special touches–here advising a change in a muralist's colors to make sure they would be compatible with the tone of the limestone; there suggesting a change in altar furnishings so they would better complement a reredos. The only area in which he would not involve himself was modern conveniences. They consistently failed to interest him. "Frohman couldn't have cared less," Jack Fanfani told me. "He was a conceptual thinker. But he could also figure out the specifics it took to do a job–everything and anything–except plumbing!"

Neither did Frohman have any concern for cost when it conflicted with doing a job properly. Feller tells how Frohman would often stop by his office to ask, "Mr. Feller, I wonder if we could change this." "I never knew," Feller says, "if he was talking about fifty dollars, five thousand dollars or five hundred thousand dollars." Once, Feller recalls, Frohman changed all the molding on top of the Central Tower by one eighth of an inch because of the effect it would have had on the tower's shadow. "But," admits Feller, "he was right."

As a designer Frohman had an uncanny ability to judge distances and spatial relationships. He had a sixth sense that told him when something was improperly placed, and when it was just right. "Frohman didn't design purely mathematically," Feller explained. "He didn't feel a design had to adhere to strict mathematical proportions. He drafted what felt natural to him, not too wide or too heavy, and it had to carry the right shadow line. It was something built into him, his mind and his eyes. And if he didn't like a piece of stone, no matter what, he wanted it replaced." Monks, too, comments on Frohman's ability to visualize finished work: "His eye is so amazingly good that I have hardly known a case in which it has betrayed him; and of what he has presented from time to time as an improvement in detail–the more one studies it, the more one realizes that it is

*Parade of pinnacles rises above the buttresses of the nave.*

genuinely an improvement and not simply a change."

During the course of his life, growing recognition came Frohman's way, together with honors and critical acclaim. Yet he continued to protest the extent of his contribution to the Cathedral. "Frohman had a sense of anonymity," recalls Wolf Von Eckardt, *Washington Post* architectural columnist, "and always presented himself as a member of a team, passing credit for his achievements on to others who worked with him."

Frohman's modesty is perhaps most apparent in the care he took to maintain the integrity of Bodley and Vaughan's original design. He made, it is true, many changes. But this was only to be expected. As an editorial in *Christian Art* explained shortly after Dr. Bodley's death: "... the published design can hardly be considered more than preliminary sketches. Marked by notable conservatism and a strictly English quality, they show, together with gravity and restraint, many of the inevitable defects of preliminary sketches."

Frohman put it another way: "My faith that the entire design [would have been] improved and perfected by revision seemed to be quite justified upon visiting the Bethlehem Chapel in 1914. Here indeed was a more beautiful crypt than I had seen abroad and the most inspiring and satisfying example of church architecture in America. The improvement in the executed structure over the original design for the interior of the Chapel was so great that it seemed reasonable to believe that this same refining process would pervade the revision of the entire design. The magnificence of the site of the Cathedral thrilled me, and while walking about the grounds, I could see in my mind's eye a vision of the Cathedral completed–the same Cathedral shown in the original design but glorified and perfected."

With neither Bodley nor Vaughan any longer available to proceed with the "refining process," it became Frohman's task to realize their plans for the Cathedral "but glorified and perfected."

Bodley and Vaughan's preliminary plans envisioned a predominantly English Gothic structure; under Frohman's guidance the style became more eclectic, a happy blending of Medieval Gothic from both England and the Continent. Like the English cathedral at Canterbury, which was built by a French architect and so is a meld of English and French styles, Frohman's cathedral combines architectural elements from both sides of the North Sea. His crypt chapels, designed between 1919 and 1922, are believed to be the first structures of Norman design since the eleventh century. The development of his ideas for these unusual chapels can best be described in his own words: "In autumn of 1922 I visited Mont-Saint-Michel. Among the

13

many features ... that impressed me was the Crypt des Gros Piliers [of the Abbey]. The Gros Piliers were massive round piers ... although of 15th century architecture, they were larger than any of the Norman piers in the crypt of Mont-Saint-Michel itself. They caused me to desire to build some huge round piers in the crypt of the Cathedral ... piers much larger than the Gros Piliers of the Abbey of Mont-Saint-Michel.

"In the spring of 1925, while inspecting the progress of work on the foundation beneath the Crossing, I saw in my mind's eye the picture of an impressive chapel with the largest round piers in the world. They would support the Central Tower and be four or five times the diameter of the Gros Piliers ... an unrivaled opportunity to build a unique and singularly impressive chapel.

*Part of the sedilia frames a brick from the original Jamestown colony, 1607.*

"I told Dean Bratenahl of my dream. He asked me to submit sketches, which I did, with the result that the Building Committee and the Chapter approved the idea and I was instructed to prepare working drawings and detail drawings for cut stone with all haste possible so the adjacent construction would not be held up.

"The architectural style of the chapel might be designated as round and pointed Norman–a transition between Norman and early Gothic. However, it was not designed to conform to any historic style, but rather with the desire that it should be a sound and logical expression of its structural function and that it should fulfill the spiritual purpose for which it was created."

G. Gardner Monks, commenting on Frohman's ability to work creatively within the medium of Gothic architecture, says, "I have watched Mr. Frohman long enough and worked with him enough to realize how he uses the Gothic medium to express in new and creative ways some of the deepest aspirations of the human spirit. As an example of his originality might be cited this instance: the four bays where the transept and the main body of the church intersect present peculiar problems. Because of the large piers of the crossing, they are not squares. This poses a complicated and difficult technical problem. Mr. Frohman worked out four completely separate answers to this problem in his treatment of the four piers involved. Some of these treatments are entirely without architectural precedent ... His conception and treatment of the Chapel of St. Joseph of Arimathea is a genuinely original creation."

It is in the crypt that contains the Chapel of St. Joseph of Arimathea that Frohman placed the four pillars, each twenty-seven feet in diameter, which surpass in size the Gros Piliers of Mont-Saint-Michel.

Frohman's south transept entrance, with its portal arches, draws upon Spanish Gothic,

*A network of scaffolding rises with the west facade, still under construction in 1978.*

whereas the north porch, retaining much of Bodley's original scheme, is mostly English.

Frohman added greatly to the richness of detail in the Cathedral's interior, almost doubling the number of bosses and adding far more embellishments of every description. In doing so, he reiterated the idea of a "national" church: "...it would be well, in some parts of the Cathedral," he wrote, "if place could be made for statues, bas-reliefs, and other works commemorating great American heroes and statesmen of the United States, and historical incidents of Colonial times and after the Revolution, which are dear to the hearts of the American people. This could be easily arranged and suitable places found." How well he succeeded can be seen in the subjects chosen for the many statues,

stained-glass windows, carvings, kneeling cushions, and various other decorative elements which greet the eye at every turn.

The west end, the only section of the Cathedral that remains to be completed, is said to be the culmination of Frohman's genius–his most plastic work and his most original design. It is all the more exciting because the Building Committee decided to break with tradition, choosing "Creation" as the theme for this part of the Cathedral instead of the more usual "Last Judgment." And it was the Committee's liberal interpretation of "Creation" that enabled stained-glass artist Rowan LeCompte to win their approval of his spectacular west rose window. Their open-mindedness was further in evidence when they approved Rick Hart's

15

fluid sculptures depicting the metamorphosis of "Creation."

It was in the west end that Frohman made the most extensive changes in the original plans. "A careful analysis of the [original] design," he wrote in 1921, "reveals the following:

"1. The whole front has a narrow, constricted appearance which is not suggestive of such an ample and well-proportioned nave and aisles as shown in the design.

"2. The three great arched openings of the porch are not well related to each other. They do not form an harmonious and satisfying composition. The central arch is too low, while the flanking arches are too high and narrow.

"3. The towers are too narrow and are not correctly proportioned to the whole mass of the Cathedral.

"4. The buttresses do not produce a sufficient effect of strength and repose.

"5. There is insufficient balance between vertical and horizontal lines of shadow. The front is lacking in horizontals and is not sufficiently tied in and related to the lines of the clerestory and aisles. In an effort to produce an effect of verticality and height, horizontal string courses and subdivisions into stories have been omitted from the towers. In actual execution this will tend to diminish the apparent height of the towers, because the eye will have almost no measure of height which will enable it to grasp the actual altitude of the towers.

"6. The towers seem to be standing on slender legs flanking the nave, and seem almost to lean toward each other in order to obtain mutual support. This diminishes the calm repose and apparent stability of the western front.

"7. The facade lacks a great western window. The small wheel window in the original design seems inadequate and from the interior would be rather insignificant.

"The sum total of these features is to produce a west front which seems lacking in that beauty and grandeur which should be possessed by the facade of such a great Cathedral.

"In order to make this criticism constructive, let us ascertain the means by which the west front can be made to produce that satisfying result which its creators must have had in mind.

"1. The constricted effect of the west front can be overcome by placing the towers a trifle further apart and by a slight widening of the towers. Reference to comparative floor plans we have prepared will show that in the revised plan the total width across the tower buttresses is greater than the total width across aisle buttresses. This second plan at the first glance looks more like the plan of a typical cathedral with western towers.

"2. The arches should be brought into proper relation by raising the central arch and porch vaulting up to the level of the nave vaulting, while the flanking arches should be dropped to the level of the aisle vaulting. The arches should also be increased in width so that the ratio of height to span will be the same in the three arches. It will then be found that the three arches are perfectly related both to each other and also to the whole structure. They will be a frank and logical expression of the nave and aisles and will produce the same satisfying beauty as does the cross section through nave and aisles.

"3. The towers should be widened and their height increased in proportion. This will not only increase the beauty and impressiveness of the front, but it will improve the composition of the Cathedral from every point of view. There is a certain geometrical relation which should always determine the height and width of towers in relation to the height and width of a nave. This is no matter of guess work or personal taste; it is just as

*The roof of the nave, with flying buttresses on either side. Construction of the west front can be seen at top of picture.*

much a matter of law as are the rules of harmony in music. The application of mathematics to architecture does not tend to lessen the spiritual and emotional value of a structure any more than does the knowledge of harmony rob a composer of his ability to produce soul-stirring music....

"4. An increase in the projection of the buttresses and a proper readjustment of the location and nature of the offsets will produce the proper diminution and increase the grace and stability of the towers and west front.

"5. The proper balance between vertical and horizontal lines will be given by the introduction of string courses and arcading at the right levels. In order to tie the front into the structure, the levels of horizontals should be determined by the height of the triforium floor, the level of the internal clerestory string course and external balustrade. The introduction of arcading, which is so typical in medieval towers, will give the eye the necessary unit of measure, and will increase the apparent height of the towers and will give better scale to the entire facade.

"6. Repose and stability will be attained by the above-mentioned string courses and arcading and by the increase in the mass of masonry supporting the corners of the towers and adjacent to the nave, which the widening of the facade will make possible.

"7. Raising the central arch and vault makes possible the much-needed western rose window. Such a great window is characteristic of the finest Gothic Cathedral facades and is one of the glories of the interior...."

Even after he had converted these carefully considered changes into drawings, Frohman was not completely content. "I do not feel," he wrote, "that the ideal solution to the west front has yet been attained. Further study may reveal the fact that a more beautiful and satisfactory result may be obtained."

Although the west facade–the main entrance to the Cathedral–still lacks completed towers, its imposing beauty greets the visitor with all the majesty and grace that Frohman could have hoped for. Once inside, the west rose window blazes in beauty high above the nave, illuminating the Indiana limestone with brilliant, ever-changing colors. Everywhere throughout the Cathedral are the myriad details and subtle touches that reveal Frohman's hand and skill. The *Washington Post*, in an interview with Frohman when he was eighty, tried to describe his many talents; "Trained for years in the Gothic architecture centers of Europe, he is a specialist in the structural engineering of cathedrals. He is an authority on Romanesque and Gothic design, on ecclesiastical art, on stained glass, on the design and voicing of organs, on the physics of music...."

Frohman devoted over fifty years of his life to the Cathedral. At the time of his death he was still hard at work upon the drawings of the interior details. Today he rests in a site he would surely have wished for: he is one of the chosen few to be interred within the Cathedral proper.

After the death of Bishop Satterlee, Alfred Harding became the second Bishop of Washington, from 1909 until 1923. Toward the end of 1923, James Edward Freeman was named the new bishop. Working with Dean Bratenahl and the Building Committee, Freeman finished, by the fall of 1929, the iconography for both the north transept and the north choir chapel section. John J. Pershing, who had served as General of the American Armies during World War I, had recently become chairman of the National Cathedral Association, and the building began to receive increased attention across the country. The New York *Evening Post* reported that General Pershing planned to make the construction of the Cathedral his "chief interest ... as a soldier rather than as a religionist."

As the Depression deepened, Bishop

Freeman tried to keep as many craftsmen as possible employed, and did what he could to further the Cathedral's construction. In 1943 Bishop Freeman died; World War II preoccupied the nation, and work at the Cathedral had slowed to a virtual state of suspension. This condition was to last for the next seven years.

Building began again in earnest in 1951. For the next twenty-five years, from 1951 to 1977, Francis Sayre, as Dean and chairman of the Building Committee, led the National Cathedral during its period of greatest construction. It is largely owing to him that the Cathedral has both a central tower and a completed nave. And it has been Dean Sayre in his role as Chief Iconographer who has developed the character of the embellishments–one of the most important aspects of the Cathedral's design. "Trying to communicate emotion," Sayre told me, "is a profession that no one in America really knows about. The Cathedral attempts to do this through its stone, its glass, its metal and its music. But it is a very difficult and subjective task. I wish I knew ten times as much history and literature because then I could have woven an even richer fabric. Iconography involves the senses as well as the mind. Art should be both rational and emotional, I venture to think. And so should iconography."

Like Frohman, Dean Sayre was more concerned with maintaining quality than with getting the job done as quickly and as cheaply as possible. As chairman of the Building Committee, he served as a practical, guiding administrator. He made necessary compromises while still adhering to the highest standards. When I asked the Dean if the purpose for building the Cathedral was as strong today as when it was originally conceived, he responded without hesitation. "Absolutely. We are building an instrument that can be far more eloquent and permanent than all the sermons in the world. It is an

(Left to right) *Clyde C. Roth, Philip Frohman, and Dean Francis Sayre go over plans for the central tower.*

uphill fight today, just as it was then, and there are fewer trained to do the work. But was it ever more worth doing than today–in this new world, this 'nuclear' age. The twentieth century has too few spokesmen–this is a spokesman."

Francis Sayre's first visit to the Cathedral took place when he was a child. He recalls a pleasant drive up Embassy Row in a Pierce-Arrow, beside his grandfather, President Woodrow Wilson. As a boy, from the time he was ten years old, Sayre spent his summers in Europe, touring cathedrals of the Continent with his parents, who were great admirers of the Gothic style. When Sayre became Dean shortly after the end of World War II, only the apse, choir, and north transept had been built; the crossing was not yet completed and there was no central tower or nave. The greatest part still remained to be

19

*The exterior of the apse.*

done. Dean Sayre served as a catalyst, galvanizing the staff back into action after the long slowdown which had started during the Depression and had lasted through the war. In a relatively short time construction was back in full swing.

Sayre saw his work with the Building Committee as the central focus of his efforts. "The Cathedral is an embroidery of many arts, many crafts, and many skills. I see the Building Committee as the weaver of that embroidery. We are building in a modern age, so we have people who know the technical side of our construction, as well as those who understand union labor, nonunion labor, and contractors. But we also need advisers who know what can be done with metal, with stained glass, and with stone. We need those who understand art. And from such people, several of each, because no one is unerring, and they help to balance each other. From all this comes a consensus that is as close to perfect in design and execution as is humanly possible. We should not settle for less than the finest we know how to produce; that is the idea we have tried to adhere to. I consider this to be a Cathedral of total honesty–no shortcuts–in this age which doesn't build this way. To do this some say is impossible in these times; it is hardly even attempted. And there are many other problems. Just consider the problem of trying to coordinate the work of a sculptor whose integrity and genius is very great and all his own–on his way up in

20

the modern world. And think of asking this man, this individualist, to tailor and design his sculpture so that it fits within an architecture of another genius, whose work is much larger. We have many sessions where the sculptor says, I believe this, and the architect says, I believe that—and they just don't jibe. It may come down to a section of molding, the transition from the sculptured stone to the architectural element, the column or the wall. Each artist has his own feeling about how it should be. Where is the borderline? Whose point of view prevails? The Building Committee has to coordinate this process and often must, in the final analysis, act as a jury. It's not easy, but we continue to pay no attention to the world's standards, only to our own."

Once the Committee votes its approval it becomes the job of Richard Feller, the Cathedral's Clerk of the Works, to implement its decision. Feller describes his responsibility: "to carry out the mandates, the decisions, and the hopes of the Building Committee." Feller's assistant, Jack Fanfani, says, "Our work is a little bit of everything, from contracts and accounting to working directly with the craftsmen, helping them do their assignments and controlling the quality of anything that is to become a part of the Cathedral." Like Frohman and Sayre, Feller is a perfectionist, but he is, in his own words, "a hard-nosed realist" as well. Feller translates the ideals of quality set forth by the Committee into the "real thing." And like Frohman, Sayre, and Jack Fanfani, Richard Feller seems a man molded exactly for the position he holds.

Richard Feller first came to Washington after working in his father's business in Martinsburg, West Virginia. He was a trained engineer and already had a great deal of on-the-job experience before joining the Cathedral's staff. "The trouble with engineering," Feller told me, "is that most of the buildings being constructed are meant to stand for twenty-five years; if they don't fall down by then, they are expected to be demolished. When I first heard Dean Sayre talk about the Cathedral at Trinity Church in Maryland, what he said set me on fire and I made an appointment to see him. The next thing I knew, I decided to take a cut in salary and go to work on the Cathedral's staff."

Although he had previously been working as an engineer, Feller spent his first years at the Cathedral in the business office, drawing upon his experience with architecture, cost accounting, and construction management. He succeeded in streamlining the Cathedral's purchasing system and in reorganizing the business side of construction, bringing it up to date and making it more efficient. One of his first assignments was a request from Dean Sayre to look into the quality and price of the limestone the Cathedral was buying. He found the quality to be excellent, but when the next contract was signed, Feller was able to save the Cathedral nearly $200,000. Once, on a trip to England when Feller was visiting Bath, his eye was caught by a Linden crane. At that time a Linden crane was a very advanced type of hoist, much more versatile than those com-

*Foliated shadow of a pinnacle on the lead roof of the apse.*

monly used. He examined it carefully, and, as a result of his report on it, the Cathedral became the second construction project in North America to employ the Linden crane. Fanfani told me that builders from all over the United States traveled to the Cathedral to inspect it and were soon ordering it themselves. "Gothic builders that we are," Fanfani said, "we have given the modern construction industry a tip or two!"

Now, in addition to his many and varied responsibilities as Clerk of the Works, Feller is also secretary of the Building Committee and assistant to the Chief Iconographer. As a further example of his versatility, Feller has made iconography another area of his expertise.

Though he has been at the Cathedral long enough "to retire to West Virginia and run a store I have there," Feller says he has decided to stay on as Clerk of the Works "because I am one of the last around who can supervise Gothic construction." While construction of the west towers has been stopped temporarily by a shortage of funds, Feller is hopeful that work will begin again, and that the Cathedral will be completed. Meanwhile he continues to serve as adviser to the Committee for the work already commissioned.

Jack Fanfani, Assistant Clerk of the Works, has shared Feller's responsibilities and in the course of this has acquired both the theoretical and the practical knowledge of building a Gothic cathedral. He has worked with the artists in stone, glass, metal, and tile, and no man at the Cathedral has a broader background in the Gothic crafts. His job, he told me, "requires that I have a knowledge of what is right and what is wrong in each of the crafts. The only way to develop a real understanding of the work is by doing it."

Both Fanfani's father and his uncle were cathedral carvers and sculptors. His father wanted him to be a sculptor rather than a carver, but Fanfani would sneak into the carvers' shop and practice chipping stone as soon as he could handle the heavy tools. After graduating from the Carnegie Institute of Technology in Pittsburgh, Fanfani worked for a time as a professional stone carver. He then was employed as a commercial artist and later as a free-lance stained-glass designer. Eventually he became a partner in a stained-glass studio and began working as both a fabricator and a designer. It was a small firm, and when the founder died, Fanfani began another career, in sheet metal and wrought iron–crafts that he afterward taught in the Virginia public schools. (Fanfani earlier had owned a cabinetmaking shop and also completed course work for master's degrees in the industrial arts.) One Christmas vacation, while still a teacher, Fanfani went to work at the Cathedral doing some odds and ends of stone carving. This vacation changed the course of his life and he never returned to the classroom.

In 1957, when building funds ran short and carving was more or less suspended, Fanfani joined the Clerk of the Works staff. He says it is the most satisfying job he has ever had because it enables him to draw upon so many facets of his diverse experience. "Often I can compensate for gaps that appear in the areas where the artists of different mediums converge: where, for example, the metal meets the stone."

Work has been brought to a halt several times during the more than seventy years since construction began. Most recently, in January 1978, with only the two west end towers left to be completed, a tight national economy and rising inflation unavoidably forced the Cathedral into debt. Richard Wayne Dirksen, present Cathedral Organist and Choirmaster, talked with me about this problem. "We could see the present shutdown coming in 1971. The Building Committee's plan was to launch a push to finish the nave in five years–it was a good plan and, although we foresaw a deficit, who could foresee the upheavals of the years between 1971 and 1975. The effects of the war in Vietnam, the oil embargo, ongoing rampant inflation (we had no prices to raise) ... by 1974, when the situation we were in became clear, we had passed the point of no return. Just the act of shutting down construction costs nearly a million dollars today. We have a debt that is seventy percent greater than anything we had anticipated. And, for the time being at least, we can't go on. But we did manage to finish the nave and now the full Cathedral can be used."

It may be that time, as well as money, has run out for the Cathedral. Craftsmen in stone and in many of the other Cathedral arts are scarcer every year. Yet there is still more than thirty years' work just in the carving that remains to be done on the west towers. Some say that if there is work there will be craftsmen; others feel that it takes a generation at the very least for a craft to be reborn and this new delay may be one too many.

Most of the Cathedral's staff are optimistic, and the attitude of the workers, all-important in construction of this sort where quality is paramount, remains steadfast. There is never a thought of lowering standards. "It's so good and so close to being completed," Billy Cleland, the Master Mason, says, "Why spoil it now? I'd rather see it stand unfinished forever!"

# INSPIRATION IN STONE

Eyes bulging with mischievous glee, sharp fangs glistening in the noonday sun, the bald-headed prehistoric creature claws the terrified head of a fellow stone monster. A spiny alligator and a winged pig watch the struggle without any apparent inclination to interfere. Behind this fantastic scene a smooth-surfaced masonry wall descends, dividing to form intricate window tracery, then comes together again forty feet below. There humans pass by, oblivious to the grotesque battle raging above them. To the left and to the right flying buttresses soar crisply skyward; every curve and angle turns with the grace and precision of a ballet, permitting no interruption in the flow of Gothic lines that choreograph the National Cathedral.

The Cathedral's nave is over one hundred feet high and forty-one feet wide. The central tower rises over three hundred feet. Each of its four supporting piers is twenty-seven feet in diameter at its base, buried deep beneath the crypt. The uniform tone and texture of the stone throughout, the repeat patterns of the arched portals, the pinnacles, and the tracery suggest that the entire massive stone structure was poured from an enormous mold. It is almost incomprehensible that it was painstakingly hand-chiseled, chip by stone chip, at a medieval pace in marked contrast to the traffic speeding by on adjacent Wisconsin Avenue below. And yet that is exactly the method by which the Cathedral has been built. Jigsaw lines of mortar define each section, exactly where the masons placed it in this architectural puzzle. Closer inspection reveals the carvers' touch–grotes-ques and gargoyles, saints too numerous to count, thousands of individually shaped finials–no two exactly alike. The richness and variety of detail in the stonework is truly extraordinary.

Symmetrical patterns of stone tracery, like giant lacework, outline and define the Cathedral's more than two hundred stained-glass windows. Three hundred angels watch over the town from the outer walls, each with a different mein and one, on the central tower, sporting a beard like its carver's, Paul Palumbo. And all these marvelous creations have been cut, tapped into place and carved, one at a time in ageless stone. No other material is more stubborn to work, none more fragile. Neither steel nor wood nor cement presents the same problems; but none is as versatile or graceful. Nor has any other material proved so enduring, so resistant to the ravages of time and weather as natural stone cut from the earth. The decades it has taken to build the Cathedral seem but a moment when one considers that its craftsmen have created a structure so magnificent, so precisely constructed, so stalwart that the United States Bureau of Standards estimates it will stand for over two thousand years without reinforcement or any major repairs.

It has never been a simple task to build a Gothic cathedral. True, here and there cranes and motors have speeded up some of the work, but the basic techniques of working with stone have changed little since the Egyptians built the pyramids. Stonecutters still hand-shape the large quarried blocks to the architect's specifications; masons set each block in its appointed place with calibrated

*Stonemason Ernest Haines points the triforium tracery in the nave back in 1955.*

precision; sculptors design, and carvers execute the fine flowing lines and details that everywhere give lightness and movement, paradoxically, to thousands of tons of stone so that the structure stands without apparent stress or effort, naturally, gracefully, inevitably.

Because stonework dominates the architectural character of Washington, the National Cathedral has been able to draw upon the skills of the many master stone craftsmen who have lived and worked there during the past century. Many of them had left their homes and homelands abroad to spend their lives building America's capital city. In turn, impressed by the Cathedral's Old World attitudes toward time and quality, many of these craftsmen left other jobs to devote themselves to this amazing project. Here a worker could put his whole heart into every task, striving to the limit of his ability to prevent even the slightest flaw.

As Master Mason Billy Cleland told a new "gang" of stoneworkers, "A single block cut shy one sixteenth of an inch, or set just slightly out of plumb, will offset every stone that follows."

As for the Cathedral's planners, they would tolerate nothing less than perfection. They spent years considering which style of architecture would be best. Nor was less time spent on deciding of precisely which material the Cathedral should be built. The final decision had not yet been made when the land was being readied for construction. Builders elsewhere were turning increasingly to iron and steel, but the Building Committee concluded no material could surpass stone.

Having committed themselves to stone, they still had to choose which of many kinds and varieties of stone they would use. They pondered this aspect for three years. Marble, they felt, was "a beautiful, inspiring material but extremely fragile to handle and transport. Also, its crystalline structure makes it uneven in quality–a primary consideration because of the quantity that will be needed." Granite was also ruled out. "Granite is an excellent building rock, but too hard for fine carving and Gothic attention to detail." When the Committee turned to limestone, they knew that their search was ended; it provided the perfect answer.

Limestone is found in abundance in quite uniform color and texture, so that large quantities of excellent stone were readily available. It is also ideally suited to the carver because it has no "grain" and consequently can be chiseled from any angle. In addition, limestone is slightly porous; the freshly quarried stone contains enough moisture to make it soft and easy to cut. When the stone has been properly set, it slowly dries out until it becomes as tough as, and even more enduring than, granite.

Once limestone was agreed on, the Building Committee then had to decide *which* limestone, for limestone varies greatly in color and density from one region to another. After a systematic examination of samples of

stone from various American quarries, the Committee chose limestone from Indiana because of the exceptional evenness of its texture. Cathedral Architect Philip Frohman was especially fond of Indiana limestone with its cool color, which he felt lent majesty and dignity to his designs.

Indiana limestone was used in the Cathedral from the beginning of construction until the end of 1960. During that period fewer and fewer structures were built of stone, and, as a result, the limestone industry was rapidly shrinking. It proved more practical and economical for the Cathedral to use limestone from Georgia, which happens to have a close resemblance to that from Indiana not only in color but in porosity, density, and durability.

After the stone is quarried, it is sent to

*The Canterbury pulpit.*

the stone mill, where cutters shape the blocks according to the patterns drawn to the architect's specifications. Seventy years ago, when construction of the Cathedral began, the Cathedral operated its own mill. This was closed, however, as soon as there were enough independent mills to handle the Cathedral's workload. In the 1970s there was once again a shortage of stonecutting plants, and the cost of transporting the stone had grown so high that it once again became practical for the Cathedral to open its own mills in Washington. Today the Cathedral's mill is the only one in the area; it supplies for the Cathedral as well as for stone repair of government buildings.

Working in stone is highly specialized, and each worker has his own area of expertise. The cutter's task is to shape the stone from its rough quarried form. His work is limited to squared lines and simple curves, using a straightedge and compass, and following actual-size wooden patterns called templets. The masons set the stone after it has been shaped, then the carvers take over. The carvers are responsible for all of the freehand cutting and chiseling, as well as for translating the sculptor's designs into stone.

## THE MASONS

Once the quarried stone is cut, it is sent to the building site by truck (years ago it traveled by rail on flatcars). When the stone reaches the top of Mount St. Alban, it is lowered into the storage yard at the west end of the close–a large area along Wisconsin Avenue dotted with so many limestone blocks that visitors to the Cathedral often mistake the area for a graveyard.

From the moment these large blocks of stone end their journey they become the responsibility of the masons, experts in that most ancient of crafts, raising a building of stone. The demand for precision masonry has fallen off because of the widespread use of steel framing and cement block, but at the

*Not a churchyard, but blocks of cut stone lined up in order, awaiting placement in the not-yet-completed west end.*

Cathedral masons still use the same methods, and many of the same kinds of tools, that masons used centuries ago.

During the Middle Ages, when cathedrals were being constructed all across Europe and the British Isles, masons were held in the highest esteem. Traveling from town to town, country to country–at a time when most people, including the wealthy, spent their entire lives within fifty or sixty miles of the place where they were born–masons worked on one cathedral, then moved on to work on another. They were often bearers of architectural news and ambassadors of progress, carrying with them knowledge of designs they had worked on and new techniques they had learned.

Early medieval masons labored alongside the members of the church's congregation, often toiling in the silence of monastic discipline, as was the custom. As their craft became more specialized, however, masons began to develop an identity and interests in common, and sought ways to achieve greater independence. They organized into fraternal guilds which set uniform high standards for their work and provided special training and instruction for those who belonged to the craft.

As the demand for masons increased and they had to travel even more frequently, they often fell prey to highwaymen. To protect themselves, they set up a network of wayside havens, using local guilds to provide assistance, together with food, lodging, and stables, and even to serve as banks so that masons could ride long distances without carrying money on their persons. Clever codes and secret signs made it possible for one mason to identify another and, conversely, to expose impostors.

More and more elaborate cathedrals began to be built, and the importance of masons grew proportionately. It became one of the few means of livelihood through which a person could acquire wealth and raise himself to positions of higher social status. As their numbers increased, these newly enfranchised citizens banded together in a tight-knit brotherhood and began to assert their independence. As an organized group they were able to demand higher and better working conditions, nor did they hesitate to go on strike to win them. At a time when short hair and a clean-shaven face were considered a sign of reverence, masons let their hair grow long and encouraged their members to grow free-flowing beards. They took to dressing garishly, with enormous silk and satin capes of bright solid colors, lined with gaily patterned prints. Because cathedrals could not be built without them, their eccentricities were at first tolerated. But in 1230 the French bishops decided the masons were getting out of hand and they ordered all stoneworkers to cut their hair and shave their beards.

Word of the bishops' action flew throughout the Continent and masons everywhere promptly laid down their tools; the building of cathedrals came to an abrupt halt. Though thousands of masons were arrested and sent to prison, the guilds stood fast and, with an incredible show of unity, retaliated by issuing an ultimatum–either the bishops retracted their dress code or the masons would burn every cathedral they had built! Amazingly enough, even with their tremendous power and political influence, the bishops had no means of dealing with such a threat; the hundreds of thousands of masons, though scattered throughout Europe, were too well organized. Reluctantly, the bishops rescinded their order. From then on the masons and their employers entered into a working relationship of mutual respect. By the end of the fourteenth century master masons and university professors were equally respected.

Even as late as the 1930s, when there was still a great deal of building with stone, masons dressed and behaved differently from other craftsmen; they wore black suits with bowler hats, and they were served tea twice a day by their apprentices.

At the present time, however, the use of concrete slab has almost totally replaced stonework; only a comparatively few experienced masons still remain. Many journeymen masons, with ten years' study in the basics of stone construction, have never had a chance to work with real stone. They have not had an opportunity to build arches and tracery, not even to lay a course of stone. Today there is virtually no place, with a few exceptions like the Cathedral, where they can practice their venerable craft. The Cathedral's Master Mason, Billy Cleland, told me, "Even when the best masons first come to work on this job, they have to be retrained. They are just not used to this level of quality." And when one stops to examine the face of a Cathedral wall, it is not difficult to understand why masons like Billy Cleland have left better-paying positions as foremen with large construction firms to work at the Cathedral. Those who are serious about their trade would rather work on the Cathedral than on any other project being built today.

After the cut stones arrive in the storage yard the master mason arranges them in the order in which they will be used. Then when a stone is needed it is moved to the "pad," or loading platform, where masons prepare it to be hoisted to the level where it will be set. At every stage, handling the stone requires great care. If one block should accidentally strike another, at least one of them will be chipped. And even a small chip on the smoothly finished limestone would cause it to be rejected.

Once at the pad the stone is attached to the crane with a "lewis pin," which is an ancient device consisting of a dovetailed iron tenon or pin which fits into a dovetailed mortise in the stone. Now a rope, or "choker," is wrapped around the pins, and when it is pulled taut, the pressure binds the pins against the stone. The stone is then raised to the area where it will rest and a mason and two helpers (called a "gang") guide the stone into position above its bed. The mason cleans the stone, wetting it to remove any dust so that the surface will bond with the mortar. Wetting the limestone also helps counter the tendency of the porous stone to draw moisture out of the mortar, which might cause it to set too quickly.

Once the stone has been made ready the mason spreads a bed of mortar with his trowel. The Cathedral has always required that the mortar completely cover the stone in order to make sure that no moisture will be able to seep in later and thus soften the stone. After laying the mortar the mason places four pieces of lead, called "buttons," at the corners of the bed. The buttons, a quarter-inch thick, serve as temporary supports for the new stone as it is lowered into place, and maintain the spacing of the joint. Without buttons the weight of the block would squeeze out some of the wet mortar, and the thickness of the seam would be uneven. Buttons made of wood or slate have some-

times been used in the past on this type of construction, but the masons at the Cathedral prefer lead because of its softness, consequently allowing them to make fine adjustments in the position of the stone. These adjustments are the most difficult and critical step in the setting of a stone; the stone must be centered, plumbed, and leveled precisely.

First, the mason centers the stone with a pinch bar so that it is exactly a quarter of an inch from its neighbor. A wooden "wedge" is then placed between the two stones to maintain exactly that width. It is typical of the meticulous care that attends every detail of construction that Howard Trevillian, the architect who has supervised the building since Frohman's death, insists that all wedges must be wet when they are put in place. This, he feels, is most important because the wedges shrink as they dry, providing space for the mortar to expand.

Once the mason is satisfied that the stone is centered, he checks to see if it is level. If the bubble of his gauge is not aligned, he swings his heavy cast-iron mallet–covered with rawhide to prevent chipping–against the side of the block that is too high. With every stroke the lead button is flattened down a merest fraction of an inch; it takes six blows to lower the stone a sixteenth of an inch. "With that kind of control," explains Master Mason Cleland, "we can bring the stone in almost perfectly." And there is no sweeter sound than the ringing of the mason's mallet tapping the rock.

A skilled mason can level and plumb a stone at the same time. After he has completed both operations, he takes a slender "filler" trowel and rakes the mortar back three quarters of an inch from the edge of the joint to prevent its spreading beyond the face of the stone. When an entire section has been completed, the masons return to "point" the joints, bringing the mortar nearly flush with the face of the stones. Pointing mortar is not as long-lasting as setting mortar; it is composed of finer grain sand which makes it more resistant to moisture. As the rotation of the earth causes the Cathedral to settle slightly (as is bound to happen with so large a mass of masonry) the shifts cause cracks in the pointing which must be replaced–it is the only maintenance regularly required for the exterior of the Cathedral.

Working with ashlar, the squared blocks used for the walls, an experienced mason can set approximately thirty-five pieces in an eight-hour day. But ashlar is the easiest stone to set. The real test comes when setting the archwork and the window tracery stones, which, because of disparate angles, must be adjusted to half a dozen or more planes; eight pieces of these, properly cleaned and set, are a full day's labor.

The interior archwork is an architectural marvel. Perfectly balanced, with every stress and strain calculated in advance, the weight of the entire superstructure is evenly distributed through the arches, down the columns, and out the flying buttresses to the ground. A single stone out of line means the equilibrium is disturbed and the entire structure is liable to collapse. And, as though to lend a final twist to the mystery masons must unravel, it is the nature of Gothic arches that they must be constructed from the top downward, not, in the usual fashion, from the ground up!

The keystone, a six-ton, wedge-shaped block at the summit of the arch, is the first stone put in place. Set on a tall scaffolding that looks something like an elongated stool, the keystone is positioned exactly where it will be when the archwork is completed. When the keystone is in place, wooden forms are constructed and put in place along the lines the arches will follow from the keystone to the caps of the columns. The arch stones are then set along these forms until they support all sides of the keystone. When the

mortar is thoroughly set, the masons take away the wood supports. If they have done their job correctly, the arch stands on its own. With the arches completed, more wooden forms are erected to span the area between the ribs. This is then paved with smaller stones known as "infill." Finally, to add strength, the infill is covered with a layer of brick or cement.

Though the masonry, including the piers and the buttresses, bears the entire weight of the roof, there are, as a backup measure of safety, steel rods embedded in the center of each of the columns. The steel is presently under no pressure; it adds no functional strength to the walls as they now stand. Rather the rods were inserted to absorb the shock of a sudden lateral thrust, such as might occur with a tornado or an explosion. Dean Sayre explained the extra precaution: "We realize there has never been an earthquake in this area–we're not in San Francisco–but if you're building for five thousand years as we are, you never know what may happen!" Dean Sayre also points out that additional flexibility is provided by the tough, fibrous red clay that supports the foundation. "The Cathedral's not built on rock, as the Bible says it ought to be, it's built on hardpan. So if an earthquake ever did come to this area, the structure would bend with the forces." But, except for its ability to withstand sudden lateral thrusts, the Cathedral would not be an iota less sturdy without the steel; it is honest masonry throughout.

Shortly after Frohman took over as Cathedral Architect, Dean Sayre recalls, a stone fell out of the vaulting in Bethlehem Chapel. This caused great concern because it indicated something was seriously wrong with the balance of the archwork. Frohman examined the problem and concluded that the arches were not under sufficient pressure from the weight of the ceiling. The cause, he decided, was that somehow steel rods had

*Stone arches in the west end during construction, before completion of vaulting and carving.*

been improperly installed and were bearing some of the weight. Hoping his diagnosis was correct, Frohman had the rods cut. When the additional compression was transferred to the masonry, the problem was solved.

The Clerk of the Works and the architect are the Cathedral's quality control experts. Frohman would occasionally have stones lifted out of their settings at random, to make certain the beds, and even the lewis pin holes, were completely covered with mortar. Cleland recalls an occasion in the early 1950s when he first went to work at the Cathedral. "Mr. Frohman came wandering by where we were setting the foundation stone for the south transept. Looking over our work for only a few moments, he said, "Gentlemen, that stone will have to come out of there." And, as always, he explained why. 'The stone cutter has made a mistake and cut too much off the molding. As it is, it will not throw the proper shadow.' We measured it and I was amazed to discover he was right. We had to have the block recut."

Howard Trevillian, who became supervising architect in 1972, continued Frohman's policy of personal inspection; a policy with which he was already familiar, having served as the Cathedral's chief project inspector from 1939 until Frohman's death.

To date there have been four Master Masons at the Cathedral. The first was an Irishman named Fred Conner. He was followed by Scotsman Alec Ewan, who was in turn succeeded by Edward Fall. Then came Billy Cleland, Master at the present time.

In the early 1950s when the Cathedral ran into one of its periodic shortages of funds, Ewan was the only mason retained on the Cathedral's staff. In 1960 building was again resumed. At that time, as Richard Feller told me, "Ewan was the only one around who knew how to build Gothic stonework. I had never superintended this sort of construction before; all the old-timers were gone; it was up to Alec to show us how to proceed."

Today Billy Cleland finds himself in much the same situation as Ewan. Cleland, who was trained by Ewan, is the sole mason left. But he is young and able, and he is confident that he will one day teach Gothic stonework to scores of talented younger masons who will eagerly leave precast concrete projects to work on the Cathedral's natural stone.

Cleland grew up with an appreciation of fine masonry; he has no intention of letting the tradition die while there is still a single stone to be set. His father came to the United States from Scotland and, not long after his arrival, married and settled down in Ohio, where he looked for work. One day, as he was standing by his front gate, another Scotsman came strolling along. They recognized each other as fellow countrymen and struck up a conversation. The stranger was Alec Ewan, then foreman of the masons who were building the National Gallery of Art.

Ewan got the senior Cleland started as a mason. Cleland eventually followed Ewan to Washington and went to work for him on the gallery.

One month after Billy graduated from high school his father died unexpectedly. The family was left without any means of support, and Billy, giving up his dream of becoming an engineer, went to work in his father's place. When the National Gallery was completed in 1950, he followed Ewan to the Cathedral.

He spent the next three years at the Cathedral learning the specialized techniques of Gothic construction. In 1954 the financial crunch forced him to seek employment elsewhere, and from then until 1970 Cleland worked for one of Washington's largest contractors "setting precast concrete, and quite a bit of it."

In 1970, at a union meeting, he ran into Eddie Fall, the Master Mason who had taken over after Ewan. "I mentioned how tired I was of precast and Eddie suggested I come back to work on the Cathedral. I immediately

35

left my job as foreman, took a cut in salary, and went back to work with my hands. I had been head mason at the Kennedy gravesite and I've worked on a great many important buildings, but there is no job with more quality built into it than this one."

Three months after going back to work on the Cathedral, Cleland was told that Fall was about to retire, and he was asked to take over from him as Master Mason.

When I talked with Billy Cleland, he had just finished building the tracery of the west rose window, a section Frohman had said would be among the most difficult stonework in the Cathedral. Much of its excellent craftmanship is due to Cleland's knowledge, experience, and ingenuity. "Most of the errors in a project like this," explained Cleland, "happen because there are too many variations in the measurements." To solve this problem, Cleland invented an instrument that makes it possible for all measurements to be taken from a single fixed point–a simple, yet effective, device that permits greater consistency in this type of construction than ever before possible.

Billy Cleland's invention may not be widely used in this age of concrete, but that does not prevent him from seeking original ways to improve construction methods; his attitude is characteristic of all masons whose love is Gothic stone.

Cleland ended our talks by saying he wished there were more cathedrals being built, more real stone being worked. "I don't know about the man-made stone that has been developed to expedite work. It is precast in sections ten feet by sixteen feet. Instead of working with twenty pieces of limestone, there's just one huge slab. It's impossible to have the same control with blocks that size; they are often out of plumb by one sixteenth of an inch. And I, and other close-work craftsmen, don't find that very encouraging. I'm glad I don't have to do that kind of work."

## THE SCULPTORS

The wonderfully carvable Indiana limestone selected as the building material for the Cathedral offered its architects an opportunity to control the line of the structure with a versatility unusual in stone construction. Everywhere you look, carved stone softens angles, rounds corners, and shapes shadows, carefully avoiding abrupt terminations and enriching the design with order and purpose.

Each of the thousands of pieces of sculpture that adorn the Cathedral began as an idea on one of the architect's drafting tables. The specific block of stone to be carved is identified in the blueprints; sometimes the architect suggests the theme, more often he does not. The Cathedral has been fortunate in having architects with the insight and ability to take full advantage of the possibilities of the stone without yielding to the temptation–as in so many great cathedrals–of excessive embellishment. Instead of creating a structure overcrowded with beautiful but unrelated parts, the Cathedral has been planned so that each carving contributes to a glorious whole.

One of Frohman's partners, architect Donald Robb, was a skilled freehand artist as well as an excellent draftsman. During the twenty years that he assisted Frohman on the design of the Cathedral, he took a personal interest in the sculpture, sketching even minute details so accurately that the carvers were able to eliminate any intermediate steps and work them directly in stone. Frohman, too, devoted much of his attention to sculpture and encouraged the carvers to add their own touches, with the result that many of the carvings are surprisingly personal and suggest the wit or humor of the carver himself, or incidents in his life.

An example of Frohman's own sense of humor is the carving that fills the molding atop the column in the southeast corner of the War Memorial Chapel. To the left is an

*A head emerges from stone under the talented hands of an old master.*

architect tearing out his hair; on the right, having solved his problem, he is back at work on a new idea. Frohman commissioned the design himself to record both a one-inch error he had made in calculating the radius of the vaulting rib which is supported by that same column and the subsequent solution.

Cathedral sculptor-in-residence Carl Bush remembers how Frohman's quick eye and acute sense of light and shadow often came to the aid of other artists. "In depicting George Washington in the portal arch of the Rare Book Room, I was having difficulty showing depth and perspective because of the moldings. Frohman suggested simply undercutting the bulk of the molding so that the scene would appear to extend beyond the border of the wall."

Throughout his fifty years as Cathedral architect Frohman offered much advice concerning the sculpture, but he generally refrained from specifying details unless an architectural problem arose. The designs for most of the sculpture were determined by the Dean, working in conjunction with members of the Building Committee, the Clerk of the Works, and the individual sculptors.

Once a stone has been designated for carving, it is the task of the Dean, as Chief Iconographer, to specify the theme for the design. Considerably more leeway is allowed for the exterior sculpture, with much of the detail often being left to the carvers. And much more of the exterior work is allowed to proceed with the approval of the Dean alone. With interior sculpture, however, once the

37

*Indians of northeastern America are represented in a carved capital.*

tor all his life. "I've always been a tinkerer," he modestly told me, "willing to try my hand at anything. Even as a child my friends used to vie for the 'shinny sticks' I'd carve. We didn't play hockey in those days, but we played shinny, and I made some mighty fancy shinny sticks."

Shortly after he began working for the Weather Bureau, Bush began his lifelong study of art by taking a correspondence course in architectural design from Columbia University in New York City. Later he enrolled in evening classes given by Washington's Corcoran Gallery. "I started at the Corcoran," Bush recalls, "hoping to learn enough about painting and portraiture to do miniatures, but I soon discovered that painting didn't suit me. So when the Corcoran started a sculpture department, I switched over. From the very start I was at ease working with my hands in the clay." At the end of his first year taking courses in sculpture, Bush won an honorable mention for his designs.

Bush spent four years at the Corcoran, learning drawing, painting, and sculpture. Meanwhile, at the Cathedral, Frohman was specifying the stones to be carved on the exterior of the apse and the transepts, and he was looking for a sculptor to assist him. When Frohman asked the Corcoran if they knew anyone who was familiar with both sculpture and architecture, they recommended Bush.

As soon as Bush heard that his name had been given to Frohman, he hurried up to Mount St. Alban to show the architect his portfolio. To his pleased surprise, Frohman offered him the job the very same day, and, after eighteen years with the government, Bush left his job to work on the Cathedral as a draftsman and sculptor.

Working closely with Frohman over the years, Bush learned the fine points of Gothic design. But in 1934, with the Depression in full swing, the Cathedral halted construction.

theme has been selected it is usually presented to the Building Committee for approval, and only then is a sculptor chosen. His design, when it is approved, is first executed in clay, then enlarged to a full-size plaster model for the carvers to copy into stone.

As sculptor-in-residence for more than twenty years, Carl Bush has probably designed more of the Cathedral's carving than any other single artist. Yet, surprisingly enough, sculpture was Bush's second career; altogether, he spent thirty-nine years working for the United States Weather Bureau.

Bush, now eighty-six years old and retired for the second time, says he first went to work for the government seeking a secure position, but that he has really been a sculp-

Bush finished his sculpture for the Children's Chapel and went back to work for the Weather Bureau; he was to remain there for the next twenty-two years.

In October 1956, shortly before Bush was due to retire from federal service, Frohman called his office. "We had not been in touch for more than two decades," Bush relates, "but when Frohman phoned he said, 'I am calling because I know I am three years older than you, and I remember you said you would retire from the government when you turned sixty-five—which will be this year. Would you be willing to come back to the Cathedral to design the sculpture for the Woodrow Wilson Memorial?'" Within a month Bush was back at work at the Cathedral and continued to serve as sculptor-in-residence for the next fifteen years. "Until," he says, smiling, "I turned eighty and retired again."

All told, more than forty sculptors have contributed to the National Cathedral. They represent more than eleven countries, including England, Italy, Denmark, Germany, Poland, Spain, and Greece, and over a dozen different American states.

Much of the sculpture portrays people and events related to United States history. Dean Sayre specifically sought opportunities to present in stone themes "relevant to Americans, past, present, and future." For example, when he was selecting subjects for four carvings that had been donated for the interior of the west end, Sayre noticed that, although the donations had all been made at different times by different people, all four of the donors were from New England and "each was a seafarer of one sort or another." Sayre decided it would be fitting to use the background they had in common as the underlying motif for the sculptures. The molding terminations above the portals portray: a Nantucket sleigh ride (whalers in pursuit of a whale); the whale itself; the famous full-rigged ship *Charles W. Morgan*, now berthed

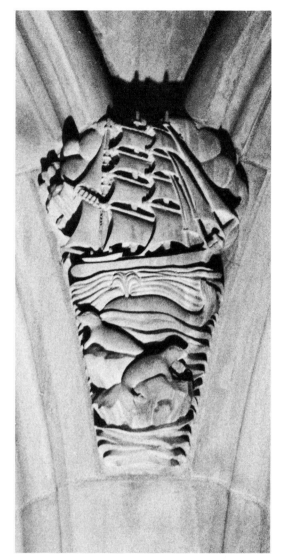

*One of four label mold terminations on the interior of the west end that depict New England maritime themes.*

in Mystic, Connecticut; and the West Chop Lighthouse on Martha's Vineyard.

One of the Cathedral's most important works, the west end portal tympanums, is just now being sculpted by a young artist named Richard Hart. These tympanums will greet all who enter through the main doorways. Hart had been working at the Cathedral for a year as a "novice stone carver in search of discipline," when he learned that

*"Adam," Roger Morigi's last work before his retirement.*
(Photo by Hal Siegel)

the Building Committee had begun a search for a sculptor to design these tympanums. The Building Committee had long before chosen Creation as the theme for the entire west end. Hart approached the Committee with the suggestion that the three arches be "combined to form a single orchestrated expression of the doctrine of creation as a metamorphosis of divine spirit and energy in its varying shades of light and darkness, of creative evolution...."

After spending three years considering a number of his artists' designs, the Committee awarded Hart the commission.

As we talked in his studio in the humid ninety-degree Washington heat, Hart told me how he had approached the sculpture. "I chose the theme of metamorphosis–planets and figures taking form, emerging out of a sea of nothingness–to symbolize the concept and the act of creation; chaos transformed into order, nothingness into reality." Like Rowan LeCompte's west rose window, which also addresses the theme of Creation, the tympanums will depart from traditional Gothic treatments. Architectural critic Wolf Von Eckardt of The *Washington Post* commented in March of 1975: "[Hart's] design is neither modern nor traditional ... but promises to bring a sense of passionate immediacy to the aloof calm of the Cathedral's front facade."

The clay models Hart has already completed must be seen in full relief to be thoroughly appreciated. They appear to be in motion, creation in the act of happening. Waves of "chaos" toss and roll, here and there pitching forth half-figures. The combined effect of the three portal sculptures viewed together is exactly as Hart promised in his statement to the Building Committee shortly before he won final approval: "...a triumphal statement of the majesty and mystery of divine forces in a state of becoming. A poetic configuration of a metaphysical reality

... seen and the unseen elements of creation; day and night in the state of becoming."

Hart describes his theme for the central tympanum, which he calls "Ex Nihilo," as "the emergence of the *mass* of humanity." The north and south tympanums, he says, are "the images of creation of day and night. Day and night, not as nouns, but as verbs, not static depictions, but events in a state of becoming. Day and night as polarities of creation."

Master carver Roger Morigi has just finished Hart's central figure–the last work of this seventy-year-old dean of Cathedral carvers. He has finally decided to lay down his tools and retire. The figure is Adam, which depicts "the finite *individual* man, the Everyman ... the concrete embodiment of all aspects of the whole. He is the *old* Adam, the figure emergent from chaos, shaped by the Potter's hand, the passion and the zenith of creation.... He is [also] the *new* Adam, emergent, radiant in light. He is at once absolutely concrete and absolutely universal."

When Hart first received his commission in 1975, it was planned that his small-scale models would be sent to Italy's sculpture workshops near Pisa, where master craftsmen could enlarge his clay designs into full-size plaster replicas. Instead, however, Hart managed to locate and purchase the large, draftinglike equipment which is used in the process. "I found the machine just gathering dust," Hart told me, "and I bought it because I figured that I, as the originator of the sculpture, would be able to do the best job on the conversion." It will be at least three more years before this large sculpture group–the central tympanum alone is twenty-one feet wide and seventeen feet high–will be ready for mallet and chisel. And it will be many more years before carvers will complete the work in stone.

Hart feels that the seven years he has so far spent on this sculpture are some of the most valuable in his whole life. He also thinks it may be his last opportunity to work in stone, which he feels, is the finest of all materials for architectural sculpture. "Gothic of all architectural styles is the best medium for sculpture because it presents art, not for its own sake; art should not exist in a vacuum. I don't think of myself as an architectural sculptor, but as a sculptor using architecture as a medium. All art ought to make a statement, a personal statement, a statement universal to all humanity, a pragmatic and real statement. And a structure like the Cathedral is the finest medium there is. ... Sculpture should not just be *viewed*, it should be *experienced* by an audience–not in a museum." And in creating the west end tympanums the audience has been one of Hart's primary concerns. "I solicited ideas from craftsmen and others with sophisticated views and also from many with a layman's eye–all of their reactions were incorporated into my final work."

Hart is very much aware that his sculpture will be placed at the Cathedral's entrance, and he has tried to test its effect from every angle of approach, at all times of the day. He studies his models through binoculars held backward to simulate their appearance from a distance, and he adds a rough texture to the edges where it is needed to catch more light and increase the definition of the forms from this perspective.

One week after Hart received the commission, Wolf Von Eckardt wrote: "[Hart's design] is startling. It is also reassuring.... What startles is the contrast between the sensuous flow of figurative sculpture and the austere formality of the architecture.... What reassures is that with this unabashed twentieth century sculpture, this magnificent [Gothic] building declares itself, after all, an expression of our time."

Interestingly, not all of the Cathedral's sculpture is the work of professionals. The gargoyles are a case in point. Gargoyles are the traditional guardians of cathedrals; they snarl away spirits of the devil and warn all passing mortals of the evils of sin. But their protection also extends into a less spiritual area. Perched in the breaks in the stone molding that serve as rain gutters, the five-hundred-pound monsters spout storm waters from their mouths, spewing it some three to four feet from the Cathedral's walls and away from the delicate stained-glass windows. The name "gargoyle" actually refers to this function, deriving from the same medieval Latin root that gives us "gurgle" and "gargle."

By 1958 Dean Sayre and the Building Committee were running out of ideas for gargoyles. So when one of the Cathedral's staff–with no training in sculpture–submitted an excellent gargoyle design, Dean Sayre decided to hold a "contest" and solicit ideas from the general public. The only prize for those whose designs were accepted would be to have their gargoyle permanently carved onto the face of the National Cathedral. No restrictions were placed on submissions, except those dictated by the nature of gargoyles–the design had to incorporate the water pipe which vents through its mouth, and it had to fit within the dimensions of the fifteen-hundred-pound stone block.

The newspapers had already given the Cathedral's gargoyles a great deal of publicity, and they now ran a number of stories on the contest.

During the first six months after the contest was announced the Cathedral received more than one hundred and twenty-five entries. By the time the contest ended in March 1960, over four hundred models had been submitted from all over the world. Imaginative submissions ranged from the grotesque to the whimsical to the humorous.

The Building Committee appointed Dean Sayre, sculptor Carl Bush, and Master Carver

*One of the many gargoyles, the grotesquely carved waterspouts that project from the Cathedral walls.*

Roger Morigi as judges, and they began the task of reviewing the entries and the finalists. Many designs were rejected because they had unaccountably been designed to be viewed from above–presumably by angels, pigeons, and other flying objects, who alone would be able to see the creature's backs; people looking up from below would see only the faces and undersides. One gargoyle was chosen especially for its unique solution to this problem; after visiting the Cathedral, Tilden Street of Baltimore designed his creature to face upside down "because," he said, "I realized that the only direction from which anyone could see it was from below." Though a sculptor by profession, Street told me his gargoyle had been "an exciting challenge, the only sculpture of its kind that I have ever done and most likely will ever do. Gargoyles, to say the least, are very different."

42

After much pondering, using the process of elimination, the three judges selected sixteen finalists. Mrs. Richard L. Kerr was one whose gargoyle was chosen. Her design was a swan, the symbol of her family, derived from the graceful black and white birds that nest near her home in Iowa. Unfortunately, although the swan was one of the few birds submitted, it had to be rejected at the last moment because its long neck would have been too heavy to support itself in stone, and also–Mrs. Kerr remembers with regret– "it was too pretty for a gargoyle!" When she talked with me about it, she still remembered the incident vividly. "It was the biggest disappointment of my life." Then she added, "It was also one of the most exciting things I've ever done!"

Though it has been nearly two decades since the contest, many of the gargoyle's designs still await carvers. Tilden Street's design was not carved until 1977. "However, when I think about the centuries my monster will guard the Cathedral," says Street, "seventeen years doesn't seem like very much."

*A guardian gargoyle.*

## THE CARVERS

Many of the creative details in a work of sculpture are often due, not to the sculptor, but to the carver. "More than craftsmen, carvers are artisans with a complete mastery of their technical craft." This is Clerk of the Works Feller's description of the Cathedral's stone carvers. "They not only understand the physical structure of stone, they know anatomy and have an eye for light and shadow, detail and line." While many carvers are simply copiers, faithfully transferring a sculptor's plaster design into stone, many of the stone carvers at the Cathedral are far more creative. Several of them, such as Constantine Seferlis, are trained sculptors as well as expert carvers.

Centuries ago it was expected that anyone who designed stone sculpture could also do the actual carving, but this has not been generally the case for roughly the past two hundred years. Today, with few exceptions, no sculptor knows how to carve, even if he once studied how. Most of them do preliminary sketches with pencil on paper, then design their works in clay and plaster, leaving the actual stonework to the carvers.

The twentieth century, with its new materials, has lived long enough to have witnessed a rapid decline in stone architecture. As a consequence, there has been less and less work in stone and, inevitably, fewer and fewer carvers. Today the Stone Cutters and Carvers Union has fewer members than at any time during the last century. If only there were more Gothic cathedrals, there would be more carvers, but sadly no more cathedrals are being built of stone. Master Carver Roger Morigi predicts: "Unless builders return to stone there may soon be no more carvers. There are already no more young carvers because there is no work for them to do. Builders don't believe in stone and there is no place to learn the stone crafts."

The early carving, which included the

elaborate niche figures and decorations in Bethlehem Chapel and much of the exterior of the apse, was done by craftsmen of the John Evans Company of Boston, but the names of the individuals who worked on the Cathedral have unfortunately been lost.

In the early 1930s the Cathedral acquired the service of Andrea Sichi and his nephew Italo Fanfani (whose son John is now Assistant Clerk of the Works). Together, Sichi and Fanfani, joined by Luca Petrini, carved the keystone bosses in the great choir and in the choir chapels of St. John and St. Mary. Sichi was no longer a young man when he went to work on the Cathedral, but he produced a sizable volume of work; in addition to the many bosses, he carved much of Bush's intricate designs for the vaulting of the Children's Chapel.

After the death of Sichi, Fanfani continued carving alone, creating both the plaster models and the stonework for the sculpture on the north porch. Fanfani died unexpectedly at the age of fifty-eight before he could do more than barely begin the carving of the lectern at the great crossing. The Cathedral then hired the firm of Couch and Haid to take over the project. Haid did most of the work himself and had finished all but the lectern's reading desk when he too died. An Irish carver, whose name is unknown, spent several months attempting to complete the lectern. He became the third person to die while working on the project.

In 1943 Joseph Ratti, who also worked on the Tomb of the Unknown Soldier, the National Gallery, and other government buildings, came to the Cathedral. He put the final touches on the lectern, then spent five years carving the interior of the south transept and the interior of the north transept balcony. In April of 1955, while carving a north nave buttress at the triform level, Ratti fell from the scaffolding and was killed. A year later, in his memory, a rough-cut figure of a carver was chiseled into the stone of a south transept stairway.

*Master Carver Roger Morigi puts finishing touches on a small finial.*

By 1957 there were five new carvers chiseling the details into the Woodrow Wilson Memorial Bay, which Bush had designed as his first project after returning to the Cathedral. These carvers included Edward Ratti, Antonio Luciani, and Roger Morigi. Morigi subsequently became the Cathedral's Master Carver, supervising the other carvers until his retirement in the beginning of 1978.

To a stone carver, patience is not only a virtue but a necessity. The forty-four angels that fill the south transept portal arch took Master Carver Morigi and his partner Frank Zic five years to carve. The work could not have been done any faster without being done less well. Few skilled individuals are willing to work at such a pace, slowly but steadily day after day, season after season. A carver's progress in eight hours of dusty chipping is often undetectable to the untrained eye. Undertaking tasks they know they may not live to see completed, carvers must take their satisfaction from the deep inner knowledge that the job has been done well. Outside approbation rarely comes in time for them to enjoy it, since it is often twenty or thirty years before a project is completed–and, on many of the higher reaches of the Cathedral, humans will never view their work at all. But it is in the nature of those who carve in stone to find their reward in the work itself. "If you're going to spend five years on something," Morigi told me, "why not work on it that extra six months to make it the best you can."

A member of the Cathedral staff watched every day for several weeks as the carver of one of the portal arches in the nave chiseled a section that would forever face toward the wall, where it could never be seen. To cut veins into the hidden side of a leaf the carver had to first feel with his fingertips, then carve a little, then feel again. Finally, no longer able to restrain his curiosity, the observer asked the carver why he worked so hard on stone that even he, the artist, would never be able to see. The carver turned slowly, and with a tone that was both wry and complacent said, "God will see it."

Roger Morigi served as an apprentice and received his training in an age when stone carving was still regarded as an Old World craft. He is considered a strict taskmaster by his fellow craftsmen, but he demands even more of himself. "Uncompromising discipline and accuracy," says Carl Tucker, "are Roger Morigi's ordinary way of life."

Morigi was born in 1907 in a small town in Italy on the Swiss border. Stone was the industry of the region and virtually everyone worked in the trade. From a very early age Morigi held various small jobs in the quarries. His father, an accomplished carver, traveled back and forth from Italy to the United States in the 1890s to work on the old Library

*Crockets and grotesques embellish a pinnacle.*

*Grotesques, caricatures, and portraits, carved into the base of finials, wait in the carving shed to be raised into place atop pinnacles. Note the nickel for scale.*

of Congress building. When Morigi was old enough, he left the quarry to study drawing at the Brera Academy in Milan. Then, "putting my heart and soul into stone," Morigi served a long term of apprenticeship.

Roger's aspiration had always been to follow his father to America. In 1928 Morigi came to the United States to join him in Westerly, Rhode Island. Shortly thereafter the younger Morigi began his career in earnest, working on a succession of projects that read like a modern-day history of American stonework. First, he traveled to New York, where he worked on several projects including the Radio City Music Hall and the Riverside Church. The carving of the United States Supreme Court Building brought Morigi to Washington for the first time. He then went to West Virginia to work on the handsome state capitol in Charleston and to North Carolina for a new building being constructed at

Duke University. In 1956 Morigi came back to New York City to carve Donald DeLue's *The Stations of the Cross*. Upon its completion, he was asked by Canon Monks to return to Washington to do carving for the Cathedral.

Morigi first put his mallet and chisel to work on the memorial to Joseph Ratti. When this was completed, he joined the carvers assigned to the Woodrow Wilson Memorial. His work on the Woodrow Wilson Bay so impressed Canon Monks and the Building Committee that Morigi was offered the position of Master Carver. Of all the buildings he has carved, the Cathedral, Morigi says, "is the most personal structure I have ever worked on. It has somehow become part of me."

Morigi's last work for the Cathedral was Richard Hart's *Adam*, which he has just finished. Now at age seventy he has retired, the last of his generation to carve at the Cathedral.

Translating Hart's sculpture into stone takes an unusual carver because Hart demands strict adherence to his model; unlike many sculptors, he wants the finished stone to be identical to his plaster design. But, difficult as Hart's requirements are, some of the assignments from other sculptors are even more demanding. For example, sculptor-in residence Carl Bush often left details off his models; he expected the carvers to use their own imagination in creating the final work. "With a crew of carvers like the Cathedral has had," says Bush, "and with a master like Morigi, I often turned a model over to a carver and said, 'From here on it's up to you.' The carvers would make the refinements. Dean Sayre and Clerk of the Works Feller agreed with me that the carvers should be encouraged to use their creative talents as well as their craftmenship; anything that could be left to the judgment of the carvers we considered would be an inspiration for them to give their work their very best."

When Bush designed the one hundred and fifty angels that surround the forty-foot-square central tower, he wanted every angel to have a different face. Rather than design all of the faces himself, Bush and Dean Sayre decided to give the carvers the job. Dean Sayre tells the story. "The carvers were not given specific instructions. We just said, 'Carve angels, boys.' And that is why the angels have all sorts of different hairstyles; one is even bald–like their carvers!"

On the exterior, where the carvers are traditionally given a much freer hand, signs of their originality appear everywhere, especially in the figurative sculptures, the gargoyles, and the smaller grotesques. When I first met Frank Zic, he had just finished carving a small grotesque of a funny-looking fellow holding a telephone in one hand and a pair of shears in the other. Some years before, the phone in Morigi's studio had rung very early one morning. Someone had called the master before he had had his first cup of coffee, triggering Morigi's famous short tem-

*Cathedral carver Frank Zic.*

per. Morigi had simply grabbed a pair of shears and cut the telephone cord! Now in place, high above the close, and practically out of sight, Zic's carving preserves the event, weaving one more strand of lore into the Cathedral's fabric.

My favorite examples of the carvers' personal touch, however, are the two grotesques on the buttress outside the Dublin Bay, on the exterior of the north wall of the nave. Just barely visible from the ground, on the west corner, a round-faced carver, mallet and chisel in hand, cranes his neck and purses his lips to whistle at a passerby. Watching the carver's performance from the opposite corner, a stone friar with one hand covers his mouth in horror, at the same time trying to keep his hat from flying off with the other!

Just below the whistling carver is a humorous gargoyle that John Guarente had almost finished carving when Clerk of the Works Feller discovered his theme. "I happened by one day and stopped to examine the caricature Guarente was working on. The more I looked at it, the more familiar it seemed. An explosion was taking place on the top of its head, a mallet was in one hand, and golf clubs stuck out of a hip pocket, it

*John Guarante carved this gargoyle caricature of Master Carver Roger Morigi.*

had the stubble of a beard, and its hat was in the air. Finally I said, 'John, is that Roger Morigi you're carving–blowing his top?' 'No, indeed!' he said to me, 'I love my job here!'"

Of the Cathedral's stone carvers of recent years, Constantine Seferlis stands out because of his dual role; in addition to working full-time as a carver, he is a sculptor of major proportions. He was born in the Grecian city of Sparta in 1928. By the age of ten, he was already proficient at copying designs from books and re-creating them in wood and stone. In 1940 his study of the arts was interrupted when he suddenly found himself in the middle of World War II. Despite his youth, Seferlis spent the war fighting against the Nazis with the Greek Resistance. "It was," he told me, "a hard time but a good experience, and between blowing up bridges I would carve." Seferlis remembers that when he was sixteen he accidentally broke a violin that he had borrowed from a fellow soldier. "I put it back together and it still played very well. So I decided to try to build a violin from scratch. To my surprise it came out very well." Seferlis feels that building the violin was a major step in the development of the

self-confidence so essential for good stonework.

Soon after the war ended, Seferlis won a national competition for a place at the Academy of Fine Arts in Athens. He was one of only five sculptors accepted that year, only three of whom graduated four years later. In 1951 Seferlis received his degree in sculpture and was awarded a first prize for his senior work. The Academy of Fine Arts, established in 1849, had maintained such high standards that Seferlis was only its 647th graduate. Once out of the classroom, he apprenticed himself to an old master carver for a term of five years. It wasn't until the end of his apprenticeship–more than twelve years after he had begun carving seriously–that he began to feel proficient carving hands and faces. "In Greece at that time the arts were held in high esteem; there was an attitude which made the artists themselves very serious about their work. Taking a job for money was considered cheap; it was the quality of your craftmanship that was considered important."

During his period of apprenticeship Seferlis had done some carving on several of the large memorials erected to commemorate the war dead; now he began to accept private commissions. "But most of the assignments," he explains, "had already been given to the old-timers, so in 1957 I joined the wave of Mediterranean craftsmen going to the United States."

To acquaint himself with this country, he first went to New York, where he had friends who had come over earlier. Seferlis spent his first year familiarizing himself with American stone-carving techniques by attending the Art Students League. He then moved to Washington to work on the National Shrine of the Immaculate Conception as a decorative carver, continuing during this period to receive private commissions for sculpture. When work on the shrine was completed in 1958, he went to work on the east wing of the

Capitol. In the spring of 1960 he joined the team carving the National Cathedral. "Only when I got to the Cathedral did I feel I was back doing the creative work I'd done as a student."

His first assignment was carving the bosses in the nave. "The Cathedral is the most important work I have done; what we build here is a real contribution to our time because it goes back to an era when there was true concern for craftmanship. What a man does with his life is important, and at the Cathedral we give ours to history."

Seferlis's stone protraits are especially impressive because they are so lifelike. "The trick is to start in your mind from the inside," he explains, "building first the bone structure of the face and then dressing it with skin." After examining several of his carvings of twentieth-century men and women on the north wall of the nave, I remarked to him that they were all very realistic yet every one seemed to have a similar slight smile. "That," he replied, "is part of my personality showing through."

Today there are no more young carvers being trained to become masters. There is too little work, those who can teach are getting along in years, the training is too costly, and it takes too long for the modern world. Jack Fanfani, who as Assistant Clerk of the Works is one of the Cathedral's supervisors of the quality and consistency of the craftwork, told me it is the demise of the apprentice system that will lead stone carving into the dark ages, for "only the apprentice system is capable of transforming an individual with talent into a craftsman and an artist."

Fanfani, whose father carved Bush's sculpture for the Children's Chapel vaulting, is himself a graduate sculptor and a former stone carver. "From the time I was twelve I would secretly borrow a block of stone and have at it. That's the only way to train any carver; give him a block of stone and let him reduce it to chips. Once he's done that, give

*Sculptor and stone carver Constantine Seferlis working with mallet and chisel.*

*Carver Oswald Del Frate.*

him another block and ask him to square it. He will start with a huge block and maybe it will be tiny by the time it is square, but he'll have learned something."

Fanfani is not alone is his opinions; the other carvers speak of apprenticeship in a similar vein. During his apprenticeship Seferlis went to the quarry every day before dawn to select stone. "Only by beginning at the quarry can you grasp the character of stone." But now that much less stone is being quarried, there are fewer such opportunities for apprentices. Even the National Cathedral has not been able to provide any formal training for the past twenty-five years. And Rick Hart says, "The apprenticeship is most important because it builds in a carver the confidence that he needs to go up and bang away at a stone in the heat and in the cold." Or, as Seferlis told me, "when you are working on a five-ton stone that is already in place, and cannot be easily replaced if a mistake is made, you have to have great self-confidence or you become afraid at each chip."

*A stone scribe incises the inscription into the dedication stone for the American Bicentennial in 1976.*

## THE HIGH ALTAR MAJESTUS

The works in stone at the cathedral are the result of the collective efforts of several generations of cutters, masons, sculptors, and carvers. Perhaps the most important example of this teamwork is the Majestus at the high altar. This is the central sculpture in the nave and the whole focus of the Cathedral's ecclesiastical design.

The first mention of the Majestus appears in Bodley and Vaughan's original plans as they were initially presented to the Building Committee in 1907. But it was another twenty years before building construction reached the east end of the choir and the design of the high altar was again reviewed.

The next step was taken by Dean Bratenahl, who suggested the "Te Deum" theme for the iconography of the reredos of the high altar. Frohman's partner, Donald Robb, followed this theme when he indicated a central Majestus in his detail sketches for the reredos. The carvers who were assigned to this project were invited before the Building Committee to offer their suggestions.

Next, Frohman and the Committee selected stone from the Caen quarry in southern France. The Caen limestone, they felt, with yellow tone, the color of richly brewed tea, would highlight the altar in comparison with the coolness of the surrounding Indiana limestone walls. Meanwhile, the overall reredos design was completed; all that remained was for the Committee to approve a sculpture for the Majestus. But the Committee took the responsibility of choosing this central work most seriously, and several more decades passed before a satisfactory solution evolved.

Between 1935 and 1937, while his studio in Florence was carving the reredos, sculptor Angelo Lualdi submitted several plaster models for the Majestus, but the Building Committee was not completely satisfied with any of his designs. In 1943 sculptor-carver Italo Fanfani submitted a design that was very close to what the Committee sought, and he was asked to build his design as a full-scale plaster model. Fanfani painted the model to match the Caen stone and set it into the empty center of the reredos, where it was studied by the Building Committee.

Before a decision could be made, Fanfani died, and the plaster Majestus was left as it was until 1961, when Dean Sayre asked the Building Committee to restudy the model and recommend a final Majestus. Shortly thereafter the Committee commissioned American sculptor Walter K. Hancock to make final sketches for carving.

At the outset the Cathedral had taken pains to set aside extra blocks of the Caen stone for the Majestus, but after thirty years of exposure to the elements, it was all stained and rotted. Italo Fanfani's son, John, was given the task of replacing the stone. The original Caen stone was, unfortunately, no longer available; during World War II the quarry had been used as a Nazi ammunition storage site, and during the invasion of Normandy it had been systematically destroyed by allied naval bombardment. John Fanfani finally located a limestone in Texas that closely matched the Caen stone, and in 1968 Morigi and Zic were put to work carving the Majestus.

The carving was finally completed in 1973, and the entire crew of Cathedral stoneworkers pooled together to move the huge sculpture into place. The craftsmen had to delve back into their memories for the technique of moving the four sections "on the flat," across the floor of the nave, and up the steps into St. Joseph's Chapel. The Majestus had to be installed from behind the reredos because it was too dangerous to attempt to erect a scaffolding over the intricate carving on the front facing the choir. Getting the four four-ton blocks through the narrow doorway to the left of the altar was complicated by the fact that the opening was inches too small.

There was no choice but to cut a larger opening. "The trouble was that the stone crumbles like chalk," relates Carl Tucker. "We broke one stone completely, but we managed to remove two others with only small chips by cutting slowly with a hacksaw." (Later Tucker expertly repaired the doorway, replacing the stonework a chip at a time.) Even when the stones had been removed, there was less than a half-inch clearance as the heavy Majestus was slid to the rear of the apse, with Master Carver Morigi and Master Mason Cleland working together to guide the pieces into place. Finally the last block was slipped precisely into position, and over fifty years of work came to a successful conclusion.

With the Majestus in place, a new problem arose. The freshly quarried stone from Texas stood out like a white postage stamp against the stone of the time-darkened reredos. Rather than wait four decades for the Majestus to blend with its background, Carl Tucker was asked to duplicate the color of the aged stone and apply it to the new sculpture. After much trial and error Tucker succeeded by dusting the stone with dry colors.

In the early 1960s there were twelve staff carvers embellishing the central tower of the National Cathedral. Today there is only one carver who is working on the close full-time. And the amount of work yet to be done is staggering. The two west towers alone will have over four thousand crockets–enough carving to keep a single craftsman busy for thirty years. Many master craftsmen speak with concern about the future of the stone carvings. But most concede that history always provided stone artisans when there has been carving to be done. The builders of the Cathedral remain optimistic that there will soon be money available to construct the west end.

# FLOWERS OF
# THE CATHEDRAL

Blooming with the first rays of dawn, gently fading into abstract patterns of lead and stone at sunset, the stained-glass windows are the everlasting flowers of the National Cathedral. Gathering light from sun and sky, they bathe the interior with iridescence as their many-hued rays stream through the canopy of Gothic foliage. Through the windows' constantly changing light the Cathedral becomes almost kinetic as dimensions, space, and perspectives continually expand and contract. The stained-glass windows in their endless variety are the orchestrators of the Cathedral's mood.

Though wrought-iron and wood and stone carvings may be considered primarily as embellishments, the use of stained-glass windows actually developed as a practical element of Gothic architecture. It was to brighten the dim, cavernous interiors that the French cathedral designers–first of the Gothic architects–devised the "flying" buttress. For the function of the buttresses, a prominent feature of the exterior of subsequent Gothic cathedrals, is to absorb the powerful thrust of the arches, which, in turn, support the tons of weight of the stone skeleton. Prior to this, the walls of structures as large as a cathedral had to bear the entire burden of the massive masonry alone. Only narrow, glassless, shaftlike windows were possible without a dangerous weakening of the walls. The invention of the flying buttress, which transferred the pressure to the buttress itself, freed the walls for larger openings. These larger openings led, in turn, to the use of glass as protection against the elements and, since the process for producing clear glass had not yet been perfected, the use of colored (or stained) glass was inevitable.

As may be imagined, the introduction of sunlight into the huge, shadowed interiors had an enormous impact on medieval man. In a different way, stained-glass windows have an equally strong impact on modern Americans, conditioned as we are to large areas of clear glass whose function is to permit a view of the outdoors as much as to let in light.

The stained-glass window is unique among the many cathedral arts in that the colored light it produces can be appreciated even before seeing the window itself. More than any other single feature of Gothic architecture, a stained-glass window must be designed to function with strict regard for its surroundings. It is not enough for the window to be beautiful in itself; it must actively complement its environs. Otherwise, because of its bright, illuminated nature, it might upset the balance of the entire setting.

Designing a window to create a precise, predetermined effect, through the medium of the light it will cast when in place, is no easy task. Daylight has few constants. It varies from latitude to latitude, from season to season, from bright sunlight to overhanging clouds, from the golden hues of sunup and sundown to the bluish cast of high noon. Because of all this, the colors of the glass are sometimes changed and adjusted even after the window has been installed.

Stained-glass windows are often designed in such a way as to strengthen features that might otherwise be weak points in the overall architectural design of the structure.

In his efforts, for instance, to give the National Cathedral its noble, stately majesty, architect Frohman gave it a coolness of tone that might have lessened the building's emotional power. Where cathedrals such as Chartres and Canterbury have very warm qualities, Salisbury, one of Frohman's favorites, is less warm; so is the National Cathedral. When Rowan LeCompte created the Cathedral's radiant west rose window, he devoted a great deal of time and thought to giving the interior a warmer tone. "The Cathedral's elegance inspires awe," he observed. "But without the warming fire of the windows, the building will be without genuine emotion. The Cathedral needs passionately blazing windows that will make people leap up in the air with joy."

Though in many respects the Cathedral follows the English style of Gothic architecture, the latitude and climate of Washington, together with the cool color of the Indiana limestone of which the Cathedral is built, makes the mellow, almost pastel qualities characteristic of English stained glass too mild for windows that must bear the entire burden of warming and awakening the visual senses.

The solution to the problem of exactly what sort of glass was best for the Cathedral evolved slowly. At first the members of the Building Committee did not specifically seek the "passionately blazing" windows LeCompte envisioned. Their initial guidelines suggested certain principles fundamental to all successful stained glass, and they carefully addressed the problem of local solar conditions.

A good window, the committee said, should not "go dead" when the sun withdraws—as on cloudy or rainy days. At the same time, the window should never glare, even in direct sunlight. The windows of León Cathedral in Spain, like those of Chartres and St.-Chapelle in France, are successful examples of the delicate compromise that must exist between art and function; they are richly colored, but they still light the interior adequately even on the grayest day. Because of its location in a region that is roughly similar in light and climate to Washington, León served as an early guide for the Building Committee's development of a glass concept for the National Cathedral. Even so, the Cathedral's windows did not fully take on LeCompte's "blazing" character until the mid-fifties. Many of the earlier windows, such as those of the apse above the high altar, were deliberately muted to control the brilliance of the glass and to give it an appearance of age. This also lent a somewhat English cast to the glass, in keeping with the essentially English Gothic surroundings.

"Stained glass should be to the cathedral what the tulip flower is to the plant–the accent and the thrill," wrote Lawrence Saint, the great colorist who directed the Cathedral's stained-glass studio for many years. Saint designed more windows for the Cathedral than any other single artist, and may perhaps be credited with giving the Cathedral's glass its ultimate direction: "...to create glass comparable in beauty, quality, and durability to the product of master glassmakers of the past." Since at that time there was no artist living who knew how to duplicate the color, depth, and vibrancy of the finest glass produced during the Middle Ages, Saint attempted to rediscover what Frohman, the Cathedral's architect, called a lost art.

Lawrence Saint was born in Sharpsburg, Pennsylvania, in 1885, at a time when American-born stained-glass artisans were practically nonexistent. His father was a well-known silhouette cutter, an art where shape is primary and color secondary, yet Saint's first interest was in color. When he was only fourteen, he went to work in a wallpaper

*Stone tracery outlines the exterior of an apse window.*

*Lawrence Saint* (right) *examining a sample of stained glass.*

store. "In the wallpaper store I got impressions of color harmony and design. My employer had been an expert glass cutter and pattern maker, and the man he had worked for, J. Horace Rudy, seeing sketches I had made at odd moments, offered me a position as apprentice in his stained-glass studio.... In Rudy's studio I worked under George W. Sotter.... His tales of great medieval windows awakened my interest in the antique system of window making...." Saint spent three years with Rudy's shop as an apprentice. After that he went on to study portrait painting at the Pennsylvania Academy of Fine Arts, to such good effect that he was awarded a traveling fellowship for study in Europe. Returning from Europe upon the completion of his studies, he moved from one studio to another, acquiring greater experience and refining his skills. Becoming more

and more committed to the reproduction of medieval glass, he began to devote all his energies to the rediscovery of lost techniques. Gradually, he became known for his excellent illustrations in glass, as well as for his craftsmanship.

When Saint read a newspaper story about the building of the Cathedral, the idea of the project excited him. When, subsequently, the Cathedral itself got in touch with him, he suggested setting up a special studio for the production of the Cathedral's windows. "Windows that will endure, windows worthy of enduring." The suggestion was warmly received, and in 1927 a glassworks for the Cathedral was established in a small building at the rear of Saint's own house just outside of Philadelphia.

Among the windows produced at the glassworks were the three windows in St.

Mary's Chapel and the four in St. John's Chapel. Upon their completion, Saint wrote in a letter to Dean Bratenahl:

"The installation of the Seventh Window completes the first stage of our work for Washington Cathedral....

"The Seventh Window is pitched in a lighter key than the other windows to throw light on the altar. It is composed of four thousand one hundred and ninety five (4,195) pieces of glass, or about forty five pieces to one foot....

"I believe those interested in the windows feel that the completion of the present series shows the realization of faith. When we started out we could not be sure that this 'unique experiment,' as Bishop Freeman called it, could succeed. Big difficulties were in the way. A glass factory had to be built; furnaces had to be invented; colors, including the mysterious copper ruby, had to be worked out; an organization had to be formed. This included the securing of men capable of being trained for the artistic work, as well as experts in the mechanical lines–glassblowing, glazing, cutting, and so on. A barn had to be transformed into a studio fit for window building and designs of a high character had to be worked out....

"In [re-creating] the medieval type of glass we are preserving it for posterity. When the glass of the old cathedrals has perished the glass used in these windows ought still to be in a good state of preservation....

"The seven windows just completed are based on the soundest principles of medieval craftmanship; in their color-harmonies, scale, handcraftdrawing, and in the ironwork. There is no composition, figure, head, or detail copied from any other art source. All of the borders, backgrounds, and general compositions are original....

"The red used has essentially the same color and structure as the best twelfth and thirteenth century reds, having many layers of red through the body with a layer, or

layers, of yellowish or greenish white to enrich and soften the shade....

"All of the ironwork is of Swedish Charcoal Wrought Iron, welded in one piece at the Cathedral. It is the same type as that used in medieval times....

"The lead contains tin to make it strong and weather resisting. Its composition is based on analyses of medieval lead....

"The paint, which I developed after hundreds of experiments while employed by Mr. Pitcairn, who gave me verbal permission to use it on the work for Washington Cathedral, is of the type used in medieval times. I claim that this paint approximates the ancient paint in its surface color, and texture. The molecular construction under the microscope is practically identical....

"The paint has all been fired in a muffle kiln, which keeps out practically all the fumes of the flames. The firing takes about five hours, cooling down about sixteen hours....

"Each piece has had five artistic operations–the painting–front delicate film–application of golden texture–spattered olive texture–and texture on the back. On backgrounds, which have no tracing, a wriggly line is painted around the outside of each piece to soften it into the lead....

"The cement used is from a receipt of Mr. J. Horace Rudy, who used it successfully for many years....

"Most of the figures from these windows were drawn from life, and the models selected with great care. In the miracle windows the draperies were drawn from draped figures, using garments specially made for this work....

"The type for the head of Christ, for which you had such high ideals, was arrived at after long conferences and many studies had been made. New technical processes were developed for the production of this head. Each Christ head had to be fired three times....

"Gothic refinements, such as changing the size of the figure panels as the top of the window is reached, have been incorporated....

"The outside effect of a window is important in its relation to the stone masses surrounding it, the plane of which must if possible be maintained, to contribute to the bigness of the building. Whatever success has been attained in this respect is the result of many experiments conducted at Bryn Athyn. Imagine the windows of Chartres as almost black interruptions in the stone masses instead of the lovely gray dull tone they actually have....

"When the lighting conditions are normal these windows will be *sensitive to light*. Changes in the time of day and varying moods of nature as registered in changing skies, will influence and change the aspect of the windows...."

Saint's efforts to re-create the glass of medieval Europe were painstaking and meticulous. To rediscover the lost formulas so that it would be possible to duplicate the original colors, he borrowed chips of medieval glass from the Smithsonian Institution for spectroscopic analysis. To maintain strict quality control, he never made more than twenty-five pounds of glass at a time.

Saint was concerned not only with the exact tonal shade and quality of each individual piece of glass but also with the effect of combinations of colors viewed from a distance. He knew that the perception of color changes, depending on how far away the viewer is standing, and this was taken into account in arriving at the various formulas. "Greens must be a combination of blue, yellow and *red*, and not just of blue and yellow, so as not to fuse into adjoining blues at a distance...." Altogether Saint worked out more than thirteen hundred formulas for stained glass.

Lawrence Saint's north rose window is his finest work as a stained-glass colorist; it is unsurpassed in its subtle variations of color, and in its effectiveness under the wide variety of year-round daylight conditions. Of the north rose Saint wrote: "In inspecting the first firing of an important section of the rose window, I feel greatly encouraged that we are going to have color rich enough to suit most anybody. It does not hurt to have a high aim. The subject matter is especially rich and with the Spanish influence we are going to get a maximum amount of color, which ought to give the effect of jewel-like splendor. I am hoping that this window will not only be as good as any rose window in the world, but I am aiming to make it the finest rose window in the world."

The north rose window contains more than nine thousand individual pieces of stained glass; Saint fitted them into a 530-square-foot circle, twenty-six feet in diameter. As with many other great windows, the rose is approximately 20 percent blue glass in eighty different shades. In addition, there are thirty-seven shades of yellow, forty-nine shades of green, fifty-three shades of green-white, thirteen shades of grape, and twenty-three flesh tones. When this subtlety of color is multiplied by all the variables of light, changing from season to season, hour to hour, minute to minute, the number of different aspects appearing to the eye is almost infinite. No matter how often the viewer studies the north rose, it is unlikely that he will ever see it twice the same way.

Throughout the building of the Cathedral, there have been many instances of a fortunate intervention, a discovery, at the very last minute, of just the artist or craftsman needed, or a change in design or material that added immeasurably to the whole. Just such a happy circumstance prevailed when it was decided to install the north rose window even though the north transept had not been completed and was, therefore, not yet fully enclosed. For it was barely two weeks after the north rose had been set in place that Saint's studio, where the window had been made and where, until then, it had been stored, burned to the ground together with everything it contained.

The north rose is a magnificent work, filled with scores of richly detailed figures. Nevertheless, few of these figures can be easily discerned or fully appreciated when viewed from the floor of the nave so far below.

When Rowan LeCompte sought the commission for the west rose window, it was the difficulty inherent in appreciating the traditionally small-scale figurative designs which led him to propose, instead, an abstract treatment.

Explains LeCompte, "A window seen from that distance, divided as it must be by the filigree of stone tracery, should be figurative only if the figures will 'read.' Otherwise–I am not sure but it seems to me–there is no point in putting the figures up there. To be seen at all they would have to be silhouetted very, very strongly–contrasting light against dark, or dark against light. But that might sacrifice much of the decorative unity; you would see the individual figures rather than the window as a whole. So for the west rose I proposed more of an abstract solution to this problem, and when I received the commission, the option of approaching it either figuratively or abstractly was left to my discretion. The actual subject matter for the west rose was laid down decades ago–it was the "Seven Days of Creation." Fortunately, a liberal interpretation of Genesis was approved, and the window evolved as a poetic and imaginative essay rather than as an illustration."

Dean Sayre encouraged the break with traditional iconography. "Because the message we want to convey is emotional," he said, "a window may as well be done in an abstract as in a representational form ... in fact, may even be done better that way." The west rose presented Rowan LeCompte with an unusually difficult problem; not only is it as high as any in the Cathedral, and so situated that it is struck daily by the infinitely varied rays of the setting sun, but it is also set back from the wall surface some fifteen feet, and shadowed for many months of the year by the massive stone masonry of the west facade. Because of the difficulties created by the site, LeCompte spent nearly three years evolving the solution. He worked with thick, chipped glass whose function it was to capture the sun's rays, shatter them into coruscating arcs, and toss them throughout the Cathedral's interior. During these years LeCompte carefully studied the effect of his man-made rainbows, which cast their warmth against the cool limestone to add the "fire" that he feels is so essential to the interior mood. The finished window creates an effect that is probably very much what architect Frohman had in mind when he enthusiastically spoke of the Cathedral's need for "prismatic light," which LeCompte interprets to mean "not the *light* from prisms, but the *sparkle*."

It is no mere coincidence that Le Compte came to create a window that would fulfill Frohman's vision. It was through what LeCompte describes as virtually a father-son relationship with Frohman that he was able to develop his talents as an artist. To date he has completed over twenty stained-glass windows for the Cathedral.

LeCompte became enamored with the Cathedral on his very first visit, when he was fourteen, and determined then that he would make glass for it–though at that time nothing was finished except the crypt, the choir, the north transept, the crossing, and perhaps a few arches of the nave. He recalls, "It was the first thing I had ever encountered that absolutely swept me off my feet emotionally." By the time he was fifteen, LeCompte was "thoroughly into glass" and had begun sketching designs for a rose window. From then on he spent every possible minute getting to know the Cathedral and its builders.

In 1939, when LeCompte was sixteen, at the invitation of Frohman–whom he refers to as his "guiding genius," LeCompte created his first window for the Cathedral. He says, "I was first introduced to Frohman at the Cathedral of the Incarnation in Baltimore, which he had designed. I didn't at first catch his name, but when I understood who he was, it was just as if I were meeting Benjamin Franklin or Voltaire–or any of the people you really admire hugely. I felt as if the earth were about to open and swallow me up."

From then on LeCompte virtually grew up at the Cathedral, which he describes as "a final flowering of the Gothic revival, a real expression of our time; an expression of romanticism and nostalgia."

It is evident that LeCompte, like every great artist who has contributed to the Cathedral, is driven by an unceasing passion to get as close as possible to the impossible, to achieve perfection. "There is nothing I have ever done that I wouldn't make changes in; I can never sit back and just enjoy something I've done–there is always that nagging feeling. The problem is that as a work changes, as it's created, you yourself change, and if you kept records you might see that the first effort was just as good as the last."

On one occasion, when LeCompte was informed that a window he had designed was two inches too tall for its site, he greeted the problem as just the sort of exciting challenge that makes architectural art so interesting; the work does not stand alone, it must fit into the whole. To take the two inches off the window, it was necessary for LeCompte to reorganize both the forms and the background completely; the final result, says LeCompte, was just as good as the first.

Rowan LeCompte's total enthusiasm for his work and for the Cathedral is characteristic of many of the Cathedral artists–a consistent drive for perfection and a determination to complete the undertaking. For many years now, LeCompte has turned down other commissions in order to devote his full time to the stained glass for the Cathedral. At fifty three years of age, he is imbued with the same spirit that moved him into stained glass when he was only fourteen. "My strongest hope is that somehow I will be able to finish the windows for the nave clerestory–animated, full of vitality, vigor, movement, and color!"

Though Rowan LeCompte's west rose is the Cathedral's most dazzling window, the Scientists and Technicians Window, designed by Rodney Winfield, is probably the most popular. Installed halfway down the south side of the nave, it is better know as the Space Window, and embodies the most modern techniques of stained-glass workmanship. As Dean Sayre explains, "The Space Window is supposed to reflect the jumping off from our planet–man in space." The idea developed as Dean Sayre and the Building Committee sought for a window with a "modern concept ... a window which would be a vivid and eloquent reflection of our time." The dean speaks of man's "jumping into space" as symbolic of America today, "as relevant as Columbus embarking into the unknown to discover a new world."

Visitors walking up the nave and glancing from window to window often look casually at the Space Window and then stop suddenly as though startled. Then they stare at it intently, as if they were looking out into space itself. This is precisely the effect the artist had hoped for. Not only did Rodney Winfield carefully consider the design of the window from a two-dimensional viewpoint, he also utilized the stone tracery in such a way as to add a third dimension. The window becomes "an aperture one looks *through* rather than *at*. The universe," explains Winfield, "defies boundaries and extensions. Looking through the window, past the window plane, takes one into space. Outlining the tracery in red brings it into the unity of the design, saying it's here, it's the shape you are looking *through*."

At the dedication of the Scientists and Technicians Window, the astronauts of *Apollo XI* presented the Cathedral with a sliver of lunar rock; it is now permanently embedded in the upper portion of the Space Window's center lancet.

Robert Winfield developed special techniques to create colors that would project an illusion of depth. He layered two and three pieces of glass together, working with different combinations of shades and hues to avoid, for example, two blues resulting in a purple effect. He searched for "enriched, deep cosmis blues that would create a negative-positive feeling, a void filled with colorful luminosity." He also ground out glass to create the constellations and the stars. "Much of my work depended on actually working the surfaces of the glass; the stars are ground-out flashes that break up the order of the concentrate circles that are the constellations. It's a process that utilizes little shots of light."

Winfield speaks of stained glass as a "source-of-light painting" and seeks to use a two-dimensional design in such a way that it will be immediately "expanded through its psychological impact."

Rodney Winfield started drawing seriously when he was only six years old. He began his professional career as a "visionary painter, in the tradition of William Blake and many of the Orientals.... The way I paint is like viewing something through an internal TV screen–delineating what I see." What he always enjoyed most was working in bright colors. When Emil Frye, owner of the great glass studios in St. Louis, saw some of Winfield's work in 1951, he told Rodney's brother he thought the young painter had great potential as a stained-glass artist. In conveying the compliment to Rodney, his brother embellished it by adding that Mr. Frye would have a job waiting for him if he were to go to St. Louis and apply at the studio. When he arrived in St. Louis, however, there was no job, no work of any kind. He finally managed to find a job doing "hackwork," which he used to glean experience in traditional techniques of glassworking; gradually he began to get commissions on his own.

In accordance with his belief that "an artist making a living off his art alone must extend his talents in every possible direction," he expanded his original interest in glass into metalworking, wood, enamel, and tapestry. Today, one of his banners–of Jesus with a torch–often hangs in the Cathedral. Of all these crafts, however, Winfield feels stained glass is "the trickiest because of the changing sources of light. The first time I worked seriously in glass, I was scared to death. I don't like to come up with only one solution to anything–I like to give myself options. But at a certain point the work takes over, and then it has to live on its own merit." Certainly the Space Window, with its obvious impact on so many thousands of visitors to the Cathedral, has merit enough and to spare.

In the tradition of medieval Gothic stained-glass windows, many of the Cathedral's windows depict scenes from the Bible; both the Old and the New Testaments are freely drawn on for symbols–from the Old Testament story of Abraham to the New Testament Nativity.

In addition, the Cathedral has created its own traditions, for it is the stained-glass windows, along with the stone carvings, that speak most eloquently of America–of yesterday, tomorrow, and to our times. The windows in the Woodrow Wilson Bay symbolize the most important achievement of the great president's term of office. Called the War and Peace Windows, they were designed by Ervin Bossanyi, a Hungarian by birth, who drew upon his own personal experiences of suffering and tragedy to create a masterpiece that eloquently calls for an end to all war.

The Freedom Windows (in the War Memorial Chapel) were designed by Reynolds, Francis, Rohnstock, and Setti. The two large figures are George Washington and St. Michael. Smaller panels depict the U.S. Marines raising the American flag at Iwo Jima; Abraham Lincoln, surrounded by slaves with broken chains, reading the Emancipation Proclamation; Paul Revere on his historic ride; and Moses leading the Israelites to freedom across the Red Sea.

The second Freedom Window features King David and Richard the Lion-Hearted with smaller figures of Nehemiah ensuring the Jews' freedom of worship, Elijah at Naboth's vineyard, and the landing of the Pilgrims on our shores. Other scenes show William Penn meeting with the Indians, and an amphibious craft landing a World War II tank. Vignettes of other events tie America into the whole history of freedom as it evolved for Western man.

The Statesmen's Window, designed by Burnham, Reynolds, Francis, and Rohnstock, has two main figures: Thomas Jefferson holding the Declaration of Independence, and James Madison with the Constitution of the United States. Smaller tableaux show a president taking the oath of office, the Supreme Court, the laying of the cornerstone of the University of Virginia, and a figure holding the torch of liberty.

All through these richly detailed pictorial windows, the new and the old are intertwined, as in the Education Window, designed by Wilbur H. Burnham. The central figure is the boy Jesus among his learned elders, while smaller panels show the philosopher Plato; St. Paul with Gamaliel;

Horace Mann, the famous American educator; and John Amos Comenius, who is credited with publishing the first illustrated children's book.

Other windows honor the professions–lawyers, physicians, scientists, and technicians, etc. Two pay our respects to South America and Canada. The two Humanitarian Windows, designed jointly by Rowan and Irene LeCompte, pay homage to six benefactors from our own and other lands: Elizabeth of Hungary, Father Damien, William Booth, Albert Schweitzer, George Washington Carver, and Elizabeth Fry. Windows depicting the history of labor include the Agriculture and Maritime Window, by Joseph G. Reynolds, a composition in light dedicated to the famous American labor leader William Green, while the Artisans and Craftsmen Window, also by Reynolds, is in memory of Samuel Gompers. A third labor window, Industrial and Social Reform, by Napoleon Setti, is a memorial to Philip Murray.

Often the religious and the secular are united symbolically, as in the Musicians and Composers Window, also by Setti, in which the Virgin Mary and Deborah share honors with Johann Sebastian Bach and Ralph Vaughan Williams, and where there is, also, a group of figures in recognition of the influence and contribution to music of the American blacks.

There is a window to Poets and Writers, designed by LeCompte, and one by John Piper, a well-known English artist, is dedicated to our greatest honorary American citizen, Winston Churchill. For the latter window, the artist drew his design inspiration from Churchill's worldwide radio broadcast of April 27, 1941, in which he quoted part of a poem by Arthur Hugh Clough:

And not by eastern windows only,
When daylight comes in the light;
In front the sun climbs slowly, how slowly!
But westward, look the land is bright.

64

With so great a treasure of stained glass already in place, it may appear that this, at least, is secure. But just a few short Christmases ago it was discovered that three of the famous stained-glass windows at Chartres, which houses some of the greatest examples of glass workmanship of all time, had been irretrievably damaged by "cleaning and conservation." According to *The New York Times* of January 1, 1977: "The trained eyes of artists first spotted the change; the light that fell from the three restored windows had turned as flat and insensitive as that dispensed by ordinary tinted glass." Scientific tests corroborated the artists' observation.

When a dismayed world asked how such a major disaster could have occurred, the answer was discouraging. It seems that in 1974, it had been thought necessary to clean the windows. At that time, however, there was no longer anyone living who understood the chemistry of the ancient processes. A common, modern chemical that was known to be safe for modern glass was chosen for the job, but when it was applied to the medieval glass, it dulled and ruined the brilliant colors. As the *Times* reported, "The last member of the dynasty of glass restorers traditionally in charge of Chartres had just died. At about the same time, the other restorers in charge in other cathedrals, trained according to the same father-to-son methods, had also died...." In the tradition of stained-glass craftsmen, their secrets had died with them.

# MEN OF IRON

The National Cathedral is one of the most impressive repositories of wrought iron in America, representing some of the finest craftsmen in this medium. It is not a display in a sterile, museumlike atmosphere but is in daily use in the form of gates, locks, railings, hinges, lighting fixtures, and candelabra. An essential ingredient of Gothic architecture, it is worth close attention for much of this wrought iron represents for both the casual amateur and the serious student the ultimate potential of the medium.

The medieval structure, built during the twentieth century, is the natural setting for the art of the master smiths. Often in shadow and slightly out of focus in the broken light, the beauty of the reticular iron is not immediately apparent to a visitor. Despite its bold concept, much of the ironwork–such as the formidable grilles guarding chapels and passageways–is dwarfed by the vastness of the great chambers. In addition, the delicacy of the designs of the hand-hammered, intricate shapes disguises their massiveness, bringing them into perfect harmony with the Gothic surroundings.

The blacksmiths who created the fantastic armor and weaponry of the Middle Ages were once toolmakers to all the crafts. By the nineteenth century, however, the usefulness of the master smith had declined, made obsolete by the rise of the factory system of the Industrial Revolution, with speed of production taking precedence over handcraftsmanship. The only outlet left for the creative skills of the master smiths was in architectural embellishment.

Since then many modern structures–banks, museums, hotels, railroad terminals–have been enhanced by the work of these craftsmen in metal, but the National Cathedral by definition, because of its Gothic style, actually requires these intrinsically heavy designs to make it complete. The master smiths feel that the full potential of wrought iron can be realized only in an environment of such huge proportions that normal perspectives no longer obtain and their enormous but subtly proportioned works appear graceful, almost fragile.

The smiths who work for the Cathedral designed within the framework of traditional Gothic techniques, but they also tried to create original designs that were unlike any earlier ironwork. They succeeded so well that many critics have praised their work as refreshingly inventive; several pieces, in fact, are thought to surpass any iron previously wrought.

"The iron of the National Cathedral is pure magic," says master smith Tom Bredlow. "It is the life on the floor of a forest soaring too high to be real." And magic it is that transforms the hard, rigid iron into the wonderfully plastic patterns. You can stand beside the Cathedral's huge crypt gates–each of which weighs several tons–without any sensation of being overwhelmed. And the closer you get, the gentler the material appears. It is difficult, even when one understands the fibrous nature of the tough metal, to explain how the smith's extraordinary skill can so twist and contort the iron without snapping it or losing the form entirely. If a visitor were to grasp one of the enormous

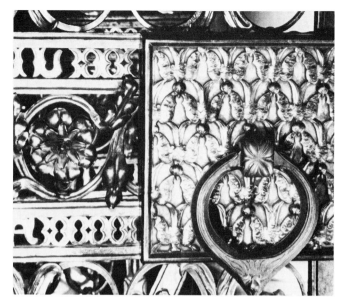

*The silvery sheen of wrought iron enhanced by the master forgework of Samuel Yellin in the lock and handle on the gate guarding Holy Spirit Chapel.*

and imagination of the smith. The iron craftsman relies on his mind's eye even when working from blueprints, for if he cannot visualize the finished work before stepping to the forge, his reflexes will be too slow and the piece will fail. Often he proceeds by sheer instinct. Subtle designs, such as the veining of the leaves that adorn the gates to St. Joseph's Chapel, seem impossible to achieve with the unwieldy tools of the iron trade. The art demands such versatile and magical qualities and a character so powerful that an admirer once expressed his surprise that "God made Jesus a carpenter when he could have been a blacksmith!" Little wonder that only rarely does anyone come along with the combination of genius, physical energy, and the strength needed to master the spirit of iron. And the patience, for iron is an unusual medium which must be uniquely crafted, one blow at a time.

Rowan LeCompte, best known for his stained glass, tells of noticing a young man who was carefully and painstakingly examining the gates around St. Mary's Chapel. Hours later, he was still there, obviously enthralled. When he walked through the south transept and sat down on the steps outside, LeCompte approached him and asked what he thought of the newly installed west rose window, twenty-six feet in diameter and blazing in the afternoon sun. The man, a blacksmith, confessed that he hadn't even noticed it. LeCompte says that the ironwork had affected the young man just as a visit to a Monet exhibition might affect a serious painter who had never before seen a painting by the great Impressionists. "He was simply knocked flat!"

The gates the young man was examining were designed by Samuel Yellin, a man acclaimed as the greatest magician that iron has ever known. A draftsman, scholar, and abstract artist of superb quality, Yellin has won unanimous praise for his wrought-iron designs. Though he preferred to be called a

bars that frames a Cathedral gate, he would discover that the surface isn't flat, though it appears to be so to the naked eye. It undulates gently like roughly smoothed clay. There is a strange, unexpectedly soft texture to the unyielding metal. Sliding the fingertips from chisel mark to chisel mark is a study in braille of the craftsman at work–pure mystery, born of the fire.

The sinuous Gothic patterns demand that the iron be worked to its physical limitations, without crossing that fine line where, as the eminent ironmaster Samuel Yellin said, "it becomes the semblance of another material." The iron itself is extremely heavy, and so are the tools that shape it. The open fire is as hot and forceful as the metal is cold and stubborn. To control the medium, the craftsman must be determined, yet patient, with quick eye, the arms of an athlete, and the hands of a painter. He needs courage and confidence; mistakes are not easily corrected–the material is unforgiving.

Few architects understand iron; usually much of the design is left to the judgment

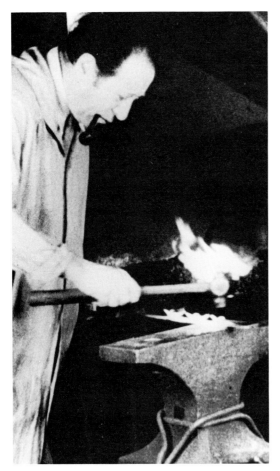

*Samuel Yellin at work.*

ancient craft, broadening the scope of the traditional forms of architectural iron. In addition to the originality of his designs, many of the patterns he wrought are so complex that even his peers are unable to explain how they were put together. So highly is his work regarded that several of America's greatest living craftsmen have turned down invitations to visit Yellin's family museum in Philadelphia for fear that their own creative drives might be crushed by the enormity of his talent. "You can be overwhelmed by being thrown into the company of a god," explains Tom Bredlow, who, say experts, is probably the only active smith capable of executing a Yellin design today.

Samuel Yellin was born in 1885 in Galicia, Poland, to a family of lawyers and scholars. By the age of eleven he was so determined to work with his hands that he rejected his parents' attempts to persuade him to follow the family tradition and study to become a member of one of the more learned professions. Instead he apprenticed himself to a craftsman in metal.

Following a number of years of rigorous training in various aspects of working with

"blacksmith" rather than an artist or scholar, he excelled as all three. Not only is his name mentioned and his work illustrated in virtually every reference source in the field, but his knowledge of wrought iron was so highly regarded that museums often called upon him to serve as a consultant, and he was asked to write the definitive article on the subject by the editors of the *Encyclopaedia Britannica*.

Samuel Yellin was exceptionally capable at the forge; no blueprint ever left his drawing board that he himself could not execute. Yellin's true genius, however, was as a designer. Employing only the basic techniques handed down by centuries of anvil smiths, he added a wealth of original ideas to the

*The entire bolt, including the snakelike handle, was wrought from a single iron bar by Samuel Yellin. The gate stands at the entrance to St. Mary's Chapel.*

metal, Yellin devoted three years in Belgium to copying medieval metalwork. He then went to England for two years of additional study. In 1906 he left for Philadelphia. He was by now an accomplished metalsmith and looked for his first job at an ornamental bedpost factory. "What can you do?" asked the foreman. A little cockily, Yellin responded, "I can do a great many things." The foreman, taking him at his word, handed young Yellin the most elaborate grotesque he could find, and told him to try and copy it. Some time later Yellin handed the startled foreman both the original and his reproduction. They were identical–except that the new piece was still warm. Yellin was not surprised to get the job.

Within a year he had opened his own shop, in an attic so small that his raised hammer would sometimes strike the ceiling; all his raw material had to be hauled in through the window. He soon had to move, however, because the heavy pounding of his hammers made work impossible for the surgical instrument maker two floors below. In 1909 he submitted a set of designs that won him the commission to do the gates for the Federal Reserve Bank in New York City. The gates were an enormous undertaking. To handle the job, Yellin built the now-famous Arch Street metalworks. As word spread of Yellin's outstanding work on the Federal Reserve gates, commissions began pouring in. Yellin had very high standards of quality and was very particular about which jobs his shop would accept; often, if he was asked to execute someone else's design, he would refuse the commission altogether.

For the first time in America, largely as a result of the fine design and the ingenuity and craftsmanship that marked all of the work produced in Yellin's shop, wrought iron began to be looked upon as an art. During the first decades of the twentieth century iron was used extensively to embellish many of the country's most important buildings; by

the early 1920s Yellin was employing two hundred master metalworkers to assist in executing his designs.

Yellin considered the National Cathedral his most important project, accepting more commissions from the Cathedral than from any other client. He admired the perfectionist attitude and quality of workmanship at the Cathedral, and felt it worthy of his greatest efforts. To Yellin the Cathedral posed an ideal challenge: to create designs that would function successfully, not only on their own but also as components of the structure's overall design. To this end he instructed the craftsmen in his shop: "A smith cannot busy himself with iron alone, he must also be on familiar terms with his brother crafts." Yellin, though confining his craftsmanship to iron, became extremely well versed in many other arts. In order to encourage other artisans to follow his example, he wrote numerous articles and lectured widely.

Iron was Samuel Yellin's whole world. He was fond of saying, "I love iron; it is the stuff of which the earth is made." He lived and breathed the stubborn metal which, in his hands, seemed so pliant. Iron was his work, his hobby, his obsession, the medium of a man almost frantic with original ideas. He was nearly overcome by the volume of designs that continually crowded into his mind. Gifted with a rare faculty for judging exact distances at a glance, Yellin was forever visualizing patterns of iron to fill empty spaces. Throughout his life he slept fitfully because he could not relax and stop dreaming up new ideas. He wrote, "When I go to rest at night, I can hardly sleep because my mind is aswarm with visions of all the gates and grilles and locks and keys I want to do."

Like most great craftsmen who work in difficult mediums, Yellin had a great deal of confidence in his skill and ability. He was modest about most things, but when it came to iron, as his son Harvey says, "He knew that he knew." Though in his lighter mo-

*Detail of the Yellin gate at the entrance to the Children's Chapel.*

*Lock and handle, designed by Samuel Yellin, on the gate to the Children's Chapel.*

ments he was a great storyteller with a lively sense of humor, Yellin was usually the serious perfectionist. The same dedication to perfection that accounts for the incredible consistency in his ironwork permeated everything he did. He was personally immaculate and fastidious; every aspect of his life–even the most minute–he controlled if he could. Often, when ordering food, he would specify, "I'd like an egg, but don't take it out of the shell," or, 'I'll have an apple, but don't peel it." And always iron and the discipline of the forge formed the axis of his existence.

Throughout his life, Yellin remained a blacksmith at heart. He was never happier than when he left his drafting board to return to the forge, which he felt was his greatest source of spontaneous design: "creativity, with a hammer for a pencil and the red-hot iron for drawing paper." Howard Keyser, an apprentice at Arch Street who later opened a shop of his own, where he also did work for the Cathedral, remembers, how "iron became alive in the flames when it was in Yellin's hands; his fire was the birthplace of his ideas."

The Cathedral's greatest architect, Philip Frohman, greatly admired Yellin as a purist in his medium. Yellin would never use gas or electric heat; everything, even welding, was done in the open fire. He deplored paint because it obscured the traces of handwork. His ideal was the plain, simple surface embellished only by wrought iron. He would never allow the metal to be refined, but insisted it be "worked as it is ... what I make must be as real as the material itself."

Samuel Yellin's contributions to art and architecture are immeasurable. He was a designer of great sensitivity who could have worked successfully in other media had he not been riveted to his love of iron. His contribution to the Cathedral is as weighty as the gates he built to guard its chambers and defend its hallways.

*A cresting on the gate to the Children's Chapel.*

Samuel Yellin died in 1940, but his spirit lives on as the modern metalworker's muse. He gave iron, and through it the Cathedral, everything he had–and he had no intention of quitting his craft when he left this life. "I shall take my hammer with me when I go, and at the gates of heaven, if I am denied admission, I shall fashion my own key."

The death of Samuel Yellin was a tremendous loss to the National Cathedral. Fortunately, he had lived to design and install a majority of the Cathedral's great iron works. The breadth of his genius reinforced the

*The crypt chapel of St. Joseph of Arimathea is separated from the columbaria by a masterfully wrought iron gate designed by Samuel Yellin.*

Building Committee's standards for excellence in all crafts, and set a precedent for perfection in iron.

The grille bordering St. Mary's Chapel, opposite the Flemish tapestry of David beheading Goliath, is one of Samuel Yellin's masterpieces. The split side guards provide a graceful transition from the iron to the adjacent stone. Closer examination of the work reveals that a single bar is actually split into eight sections, each section forming its own intricate pattern. The heels that anchor the gate to the stone floor are not so simple as they appear; each one represents two days at the forge for a master craftsman. The beautiful patterns along the top of the grille inspire awe in anyone with a knowledge of iron. Howard Keyser says: "Even as a metalworker myself, I look at those crestings and wonder how on earth they were put together."

Yellin's incredible skill reached its apex in the crestings on the Children's Chapel gates. Kenneth Lynch, a master smith himself, calls them "unbelievably fantastic," and Tom Bredlow says wistfully, "Unreal."

On the gates guarding the Chapel of St. Joseph of Arimathea, note the swelling, a technique used to pierce one piece of iron with another. "This doesn't just come with a hammer and chisel," explains Keyser. "It must be slowly and carefully worked with several different tools or it won't work at all." In a corner of the same chapel a small wooden door set into the wall encloses a row of electrical switches. Here Yellin has transformed a simple, utilitarian piece of iron–the handmade iron rivets on the inside of the door are set off by a coat of red paint, now handsomely aged.

The enormous latticework in the south crypt passageway is one of the simplest designs in the Cathedral, yet the perfect symmetry, the classic majesty, instantly identifies the gate as a work of Yellin's. Though it weighs several tons, the huge gate swings open easily, closes smoothly with a reassuring clang of the lock. The carefully wrought crane bolt that holds the gate in place is another example of Yellin's meticulous attention to even the smallest detail.

Yellin's death occurred during a time of change. The era of monumental buildings that had kept Yellin's forges blazing during the twenties and thirties had ended. The nation was in the throes of a depression, and a world war was at its doorstep. It was too much to expect that another master craftsman of Yellin's stature would appear to take his place. There was still, however, a handful of craftsmen left whom he had trained, and they continued to work in his tradition.

One of the ironworkers Yellin had recruited was Jacob Schmidt. Schmidt was born in a small town in the northeast corner of Italy several decades before the Cathedral's first stone was set. From Italy, he went to work in Russia; later he traveled to the United States. At Arch Street he became one of Yellin's most skilled smiths.

Schmidt had always been serious about his craft; under Yellin, he became so completely engrossed in his work that it seemed to his fellow workers that quitting time was the low point of his day. Howard Keyser, who first worked with Schmidt as a shop helper, remembers that "Schmidt was a wonderful worker and craftsman; he was always extremely earnest, going about his work without any sense of humor. But he certainly could produce!"

Searching for craftsmen capable of carrying on Yellin's work, the Cathedral discovered Schmidt and promptly commissioned him to create the gate for the north transept stairway. After completing the gate, he created the fittings–ten pairs of hinges–for the enormous south transept doors. Though already well along in years and failing in health, Schmidt plunged eagerly into this project, which he considered one of the most important in his lifetime. Shortly after he began the work, however, a cataract lost him

*Cresting of the Yellin gate at the entrance to the columbaria.*

the sight of one eye. Gradually the intervals between the delivery of completed hinges grew longer and longer. A second cataract left Schmidt almost completely blind, but he struggled to work on, determined to see the job finished. Dean Sayre recalls Schmidt's extraordinary perseverance: "He refused to give in until the last pair was done, and yet he didn't want to finish because he knew that when he did it was the end of his life. He kept at it for nine whole years and I had to keep encouraging him; I had to urge him to finish. But I knew it would be his last project. It was."

Shortly thereafter, just before he died, the Cathedral persuaded Schmidt to let them purchase his very first work, a small door handle in the shape of a bishop that he had made as the first "test" of his skills when he

was an apprentice in Italy. Today the bishop hangs on the inside of the slype door.

When the Clerk of the Works office became aware that Jacob Schmidt was seriously ill, a search was begun to find an artisan capable of assisting with the south transept hinges. Howard Keyser, trained at Arch Street, where he had known Schmidt, was chosen. After helping to complete the transept doors, Keyser continued to serve as ironworker to the Cathedral.

Howard Keyser had begun working with iron immediately after high school, where he had developed a flair for the forge in a manual arts class. A determined seventeen-year-old, he managed to get an interview with Yellin at the Arch Street works, which was then at the peak of its productivity. After glancing through sketches the youth had

77

drawn for his high school class, Yellin offered Keyser a position in the shop's drafting room. With much the same spunk that had won Yellin a job making bedposts, Keyser suggested that he would be far happier working on the floor with the smiths. Yellin was surprised by his enthusiasm, but still tried to discourage the aspiring blacksmith from the "hard and dirty work." When Keyser persisted, Yellin put him to work carrying coal and doing other odd jobs of a forge helper. That was in 1922. It was several years before Keyser got the opportunity to take the next step toward becoming a craftsman. Despite long hours, and a job that was every bit as hard and dirty as Yellin had warned, Keyser never faltered in his desire to learn the trade; he spent every spare moment gleaning all he could from the European masters Yellin had gathered together. Eventually, Keyser was given his own forge and allowed to try his hand. Often, as he worked, an older smith from a neighboring forge would come over and show him a new technique. Occasionally Yellin himself would borrow Keyser's forge to test a design, and would ask Keyser to assist by swinging the hammer as Yellin guided the chisel.

"Yellin was extremely demanding," Keyser remembers. "He could do it all himself, and very, very well, so there was no fooling, no fudging." It was in the intimate role of Yellin's helper that Keyser began to develop a "spontaneity and almost intuitive understanding of iron" that influenced his work for the Cathedral in later years.

"I was especially impressed by Yellin's gates for the National Cathedral," recalls Keyser. "There were quite a few good ironworkers in New York at the time who might have handled the job competently, but none produced work as fine or as richly patterned as Yellin's. His gates are stronger, with far more 'umph' than any other designs in metal I've seen. The iron just came alive in the flames when it was in Yellin's hands."

In 1928 Keyser left the Arch Street smithy and, with his brother, who had been a draftsman for Yellin set up a small shop. No sooner had they opened their doors than the Depression struck and there was no work to be had. Keyser's brother left to take a government job, while Keyser struggled to keep the forge going on his own. Looking back, Keyser feels that it was working alone that led him to experiment and build upon the experience he had had working alongside Yellin's craftsmen. Slowly, at his solitary forge, he refined his skills and developed the qualities that made him a master of iron.

As Keyser's self-confidence grew, so did his creative skills. Like Yellin he was determined to maintain high quality, and even when business was slow, he refused designs not up to his standards. This was not an egotistical posture, but a sincere reflection of his sturdy self-confidence, characteristic of all great iron craftsmen. When he received the commission to build the iron-covered door that seals the south transept entry to St. Dunstan's Chapel, there was much correspondence between him and Cathedral architect Frohman. Frohman wanted a different design from the one Keyser had submitted to win the commission. Keyser refused and, in spite of Frohman's urgings, wouldn't budge. Finally Jack Fanfani, Assistant Clerk of the Works, stepped in and suggested to Frohman that he let the ironworker go ahead and give his original design a try. When the finished door arrived, Frohman, watching the installation, declared the door a "piece of master forgework," a supreme compliment from the soft-spoken perfectionist architect.

Howard Keyser created more wrought iron for the Cathedral than any other smith except Samuel Yellin—and he did most of it alone, with only one helper to swing the hammer.

The magnificent gates on either side of the high altar, imposing barriers guarding the Cathedral treasury, were Keyser's last work.

*A detail of Howard Keyser's wrought-iron gate on the south side of the high altar reredos. Traditionally the treasures of a cathedral are placed in the apsidal chamber this gate guards.*

When the job was half finished, he suffered a heart attack which robbed him of the stamina the forge demands. "I have everything I need to continue my work, but I just don't have the physical strength," he says in a tone of quiet sadness. He has sold his tools.

With Howard Keyser's retirement, the Cathedral was once again without a master metalworker. The Clerk of the Works scoured the country, but it appeared that no one could be found who could measure up to the standards established by the Building Committee and by the many great works already installed. There were virtually no working smiths on a par with the handcraftsmen who had stood at the Arch Street forges fifty years earlier. Because of this the Cathedral was forced to compromise and there are now several pieces of ironwork that break with traditional iron craftsmanship in their employment of modern electric welding.

The work of Tom Bredlow, a solitary blacksmith in a shop located in a back street of Tucson, Arizona, is an exception. The Cathedral found Bredlow just as hope of ever replacing Keyser was running out.

At the time, the Cathedral had been looking for someone to replace a missing candleholder, one of a pair that had stood beside the high altar. Bredlow was offered the commission. Young, eager for challenge at a time when worthy projects are few and far between, Bredlow enthusiastically accepted the commission.

Tom Bredlow is a maverick, an anachronism, somewhat irreverent toward modern times. He would be equally at home one hundred years ago. Articulate, bright, and like Yellin, interested in a wide range of things, Bredlow has nevertheless dedicated his life to iron. At the age of six he inherited his grandfather's tinsmithing tools and set to work with what scraps of metal he could find. From that day on, his life has been devoted to creating objects in metal. (He has frequently fantasized about living in the Middle Ages and working in a castle smithy.)

*Tom Bredlow is front of his smithy, Tucson, Arizona.*

When he got older and stronger, he switched from tin to iron and began teaching himself the trade. Odd jobs were plentiful and Bredlow's skills grew with practice, but he always felt the lack of a real challenge; except for an occasional commission for a gate or for window bars for a private home, there were no opportunities for real creativity. The bulk of his work consisted of repairs or the making of basic utilitarian objects. "It is extremely frustrating to be living in the wrong era," he told me, complaining that not enough opportunities exist for him to fully develop his talents. "There are simply no more proper settings for wrought iron." Nonetheless, working slowly and alone, he takes advantage of every job, no matter how trivial, "to do the very best I have in me....I will not compromise, and I am never completely satisfied with my work."

Bredlow was well into his career as a smith before he ever heard of the National Cathedral. "It was a dream–the real thing–it was very hard for me to believe," he told me. Bredlow had just had one thousand brochures printed, planning to distribute them to drum up business; for some reason, the only one he ever sent out went to the Cathedral. At that time, however, Keyser was still working. It was not until several years later that the Building Committee surprised Bredlow with the commission for the reproduction of the candleholder. This was the kind of opportunity he had been hoping for. "Finally," he says, "I had found my castle."

Assuming the project to be routine, the Cathedral shipped the remaining candleholder to Tucson for duplication. Bredlow remembers when it arrived. "I opened it; it was a beautiful piece. Then I turned it around ... and around...and around. The more closely I looked at it, the more I saw and the more I couldn't figure out. It was beyond belief."

It took Bredlow a great deal of time and many trials and errors to discover just how the unusual piece had been formed. Eventually, he succeeded in deciphering the "directions," which he describes as being "right on it, once you knew where to look!" Halfway through his work on the project, Bredlow came across the stamp "YELLIN" on the inner surface of the base. "If I had been aware that it was Yellin's work when I started," says Bredlow, "it would have stopped me cold."

But by then it was no longer totally unexpected; the longer he had worked on the piece, the more he had suspected it was the work of a great master– "there was just too much magic," he recalls.

When the two candleholders–the original and Bredlow's finished reproduction–arrived back at the Cathedral, no one could tell them apart. And when the Committee realized that the original was one of Yellin's pieces, they knew they had discovered one of the finest working blacksmiths left in America. Kenneth Lynch, the authority on iron, describes Bredlow today as the "finest young master in the United States."

The more demanding he can make his assignments, the happier Bredlow seems to feel. He never settles for the easy way out. When asked why he takes the trouble to hand-fashion the lock as well as the rest of the gate, even though the Building Committee does not specify the difficult task as part of his commission, Bredlow responds, "Once the Cathedral gives me the opportunity to build a gate, I'm not going to miss the challenge of making the lock as well." As Jack Fanfani told me, "That is the attitude of a true craftsman."

Throughout the Cathedral, the locks for the gates are as different in shape and design as the personalities of the craftsmen who worked on them. Yet the locks all share a common quality–though made by hand, they require less maintenance than their machine-made, theoretically more precise, counterparts.

Unfortunately, even with so much interest in crafts today, there are just not enough functional, creative projects to provide aspiring young smiths with a chance to develop their skill and artistry working in iron. The demise of great ironwork is, like the decline of work in stone, a sign of our times.

# STORIED WALLS

Long before the advent of the written word, man satisfied his desire to keep a record of his existence by painting on walls. Early man recorded the events of his daily life in innumerable cave paintings. And after man-made structures began to be erected, pictures of various styles and more or less complexity were painted in many types of buildings, primarily on inside walls. Throughout the halls and chambers where multitudes gathered, historian-craftsmen recorded the past and present in pictures, sometimes working for years on a single surface.

During the Middle Ages, with the increasingly dominant role played by Christianity, stories from the Bible were portrayed for the edification of the great mass of people who had virtually no other access to the Holy Writ. The emotional and educational impact of these murals on illiterate peoples was enormous.

The murals that have survived are in the main fresco painting–a process of applying water-based pigments to a wall freshly covered with lime plaster. The wet plaster absorbs the pigments and covers them with a protective coat of crystals, making the painting an intrinsic part of the wall as the plaster hardens.

In the Christian basilicas, with their huge expanses of wall unbroken by windows, mural painting was extensively practiced. In fact, murals became so popular that during the medieval period prior to the Gothic era, many structures were designed primarily to shelter the murals they were to display. With the development of Gothic architecture, however, beginning in the latter part of the eleventh century, the muralist's art experienced a period of decline. The invention of the flying buttresses allowed the use of large, open areas of stained-glass windows, but decreased the wall area available for murals.

Early Christian murals bore only a limited relationship to their surroundings. For the painter the wall existed merely to provide a large working surface protected from the elements; for the architect, murals were an embellishment and sometimes served a double purpose by concealing imperfections in construction or design.

The Gothic style, in contrast with the earlier Romanesque, required that each part and embellishment, including mosaics and murals, be interrelated. Murals, previously independent of the structures that housed them, had to be compatible with the overall design.

The transition of the mural from wall painting to harmonious architectural element posed a great challenge to muralists. As murals became related to adjacent sculpture and structural forms, new requirements arose. The composition of a painting was influenced by its need both to emphasize its surroundings and to relate to them. In addition, in order for a mural to be a success, it had to retain its effectiveness viewed from whatever vantage, near or far. The delicate shades of the fresco–which had remained the muralist's primary medium for centuries–were no longer satisfactory for many of these new interiors. The problem created the solution; new, brighter pigments were developed and the techniques for binding the colors to the wall were refined. The earlier setback to mural painting notwithstanding, the flowering of the Gothic age resulted in muralists doing some of their most creative work. In Italy an important school of mural painting arose, culminating with the great master Giotto of Florence.

Today, because of the unique ability of murals to convey ideas and relate events to all peoples everywhere–regardless of differences in language or degree of literacy–wall paintings are still widely popular. They remain, both technically and artistically, different from all other forms of painting–formidable tasks of design, craftsmanship, and technique. Few artists who work at the easel care to attempt projects of such enormous scope; fewer still are able to. Unfortunately, as with so many of the arts, modern emphasis on time and money discourages the use of many of the most successful processes developed during the fifteenth and sixteenth centuries. The most common technique now in use is that of applying oil paint to canvas, which is then glued to panels and, finally, fixed to the wall. Although this method is still complex and difficult, it is far less laborious and requires far less control than earlier mural techniques, but at a price. First, oil on canvas is one of the least satisfactory types of mural, as the colors tend to appear initially less vibrant, and dull even further with age. Second, the canvas is liable to deteriorate when exposed to the pollution now common in most of the world's cities. Finally, oil paint, especially on canvas, reflects undesirable light. The resultant glare on the surface of the mural makes lighting the painting extremely difficult, and creates a problem impossible to solve in many architectural settings. To minimize this, the oil paint must almost always be applied flat, without texture, which might create undesirable highlights. Yet this is the process dictated by today's standards. Even the ceiling of the Paris Opera House, painted by Chagall in 1964, employs this technique.

To date, the National Cathedral has only two mural paintings. Although, because of the nature of the Gothic interior, the number of walls available for mural paintings is limited, the quality of the work is not.

## THE WYETH MURAL

The Holy Spirit Chapel, one of the smallest in the Cathedral, is tucked away behind a superb wrought-iron gate designed by Samuel Yellin, just to the left of the north transept entrance. But the approach from the south is best. Past the choir, around the great column that borders the crossing, the first glimpse of blue and red and gold glows in contrast to the warm gray iron, cool stone, and rich brown wood that surround the area. A few more steps forward, a stride to the right, and a many-splendored host of angels bids you enter the chapel. With hands outstretched, the central figure of Jesus welcomes you, emanating rays of gold that lead your eyes to balconies and terraces and to the spire of the intricately carved oak that forms the reredos.

In 1936 N. C. Wyeth, a famous American illustrator and painter, skillfully adapted the traditional technique of applying oil colors directly onto a wood-panelled wall to create this mural. Wyeth's painting is unusual, not only because of its use of a medieval technique but also because he employed painted strips of wood of varying thicknesses to create a three-dimensional effect for the golden rays which surround the figure of Jesus. The result is a kind of bas-relief, with a feeling of motion, and with greater control over its surroundings than a mural of relatively small size would normally command.

The restrictions imposed by the confined square space of the chapel–a space otherwise unsuited to a wall painting–are overcome by Wyeth's selection of a straightforward symmetrical design. The narrow angle from

*Jan De Rosen's encaustic mural in the crypt chapel of St. Joseph of Arimathea.*

which the mural can be viewed and the carved oak frame, screening the work from either side and slightly shadowing it from above, eliminate the problem of reflected light. Because of this, the artist was able to employ the wide selection of colors available in oil paints. To further control the oils, Wyeth carefully varied the thickness of the plaster before he started to paint.

Although Wyeth was experienced in the larger sweep of panoramic murals, he was able to adapt his perspective to this closely focused mural; the result is a painting admirably suited to the strict limitations of the Holy Spirit Chapel. His insistence on working directly on the plaster gives the mural a medieval authenticity.

## THE DE ROSEN MURAL

The Cathedral's only panoramic mural is in the windowless Chapel of St. Joseph of Arimathea situated in the crypt beneath the crossing. It is the work of the well-known Polish muralist Jan Henrik De Rosen, last of the muralists trained in the traditions of the court painters to the Russian Czars–De Rosen's father had been official painter to the Grand Imperial Army.

De Rosen arrived in Washington in 1932, the year Wyeth finished the mural for the Holy Spirit Chapel. He had come from Poland at the request of his country's ambassador, to create a mural for the new Polish Embassy. "Like the man who came to dinner," De Rosen told me, "I never left."

*Jan De Rosen at work in his studio.*

Washington at that time was in a ferment of building construction and growth; De Rosen, caught up in the excitement, stayed on, prompted in part by the prospect of creating a mural for the National Cathedral.

At the time De Rosen worked at the cathedral, it was barely one-third completed. Nevertheless, he remembers feeling that "it already compared with the cathedrals of Europe ... the intensity, the perfectionism, and the dedication of the artisans and everyone working there." But he felt the Cathedral needed murals to warm up the coolness of the "excellent English Gothic design."

De Rosen was pleased when the Building Committee selected St. Joseph's Chapel, with its massive pillars and softly curving Norman lines, as the site for his work. The vast crypt chamber, located in the very heart of the Cathedral, was ideal for a mural. And he set out to create a design that would capture the room's softly elegant mood.

The subtly potent colors of his mural, radiating from the chapel's east wall, enrich every corner of the broad chamber. To apply his powerful design to the wall Dr Rosen decided to use the encaustic process–grinding colors in molten beeswax, which he then painted, while still hot, onto the surface of the wall. Encaustic, originally developed by the ancient Greeks, is probably the most enduring medium for mural painting–an encaustic mural by Polygnotus, painted under an open portico at Athens, has survived for some two thousand years. Encaustic offers certain other advantages as well. The hot wax renders the colors more vibrant, with less glare than other mural techniques, and responds to infinite texturing. The mural is painted directly on plaster; to give the painting greater depth brilliance, De Rosen applied the pigments over a base of gold leaf. So varied are the hues, it is hard to believe that De Rosen used only three colors of paint– black, red, and white–and the gold leaf. He tempered his colors and increased the range

of tones by allowing some of the plaster here and there to show through. In some places he even left unplastered and bare the stone of the sanctuary wall itself. "The plaster was a wonderfully versatile surface to paint on; it held the wax perfectly and lent soft highlights I could not otherwise have attained," recalls De Rosen.

Because so many people find murals the easiest form of artistic communication to understand, De Rosen feels that the artist should pay strict attention both to the overall design and to individual details within the painting. "Only when every detail is accurate and realistic will the message come through." Before beginning the mural for the Cathedral, De Rosen spent more than three months studying the life and times of St. Joseph of Arimathea. To assure that those visiting the Cathedral would relate to the characters in his mural, De Rosen used as his models many of the people at the Cathedral. St. Joseph wears the face of the Cathedral custodian; Christ's face is that of the boiler man! And the people gathered to observe Christ's burial have the faces of the men and boys of the Cathedral's choir. When De Rosen came to Washington he was already familiar with the costumes and many other details of the period having spent many years teaching and painting Biblical subjects in Europe. Nonetheless, working with his lifelong companion–a miniature manikin he calls Wilfred– he carefully tested the drapery of each garment so he could draw it to conform exactly to the physical proportions of each figure. Subsequently, the Building Committee, realizing De Rosen's tremendous talent for figures, gave him the commission to design the saints to be carved for the high altar.

Because I'm basically very lazy," he jokes, "I try to do everything right the first time. Then I won't have to do it over." Rather his perfectionism is characteristic of the self-discipline that has distinguished eastern European muralists for centuries, a tradition that seems to have ended, along with the flamboyant era De Rosen's life represents so well. Talking to him in his Greenwich-Village-like studio, across from the National Portrait Gallery, I found it hard to believe that the experiences so modestly described by the white-haired gentleman artist were his own.

He was born, he says, "between an easel and a sword," in nineteenth-century Warsaw. His father had learned to paint murals in the cathedral schools established in the late eighteenth century. He achieved such prominence in his field that he received–and accepted–an invitation to serve the court of Russia as the Czar's military muralist. Jan began to study with his father as soon as he was old enough to hold a brush. Even before his age permitted him to visit the Russian court, his burgeoning interest in religious themes convinced his family that he should be permitted to study art, first in Paris, later in Switzerland. He returned from his studies "both consciously and unconsciously a painter," but he did not immediately settle down to serious painting. For a time he skipped from one form of expression to another; at one point he even edited a Warsaw magazine for young poets.

The "sword" in De Rosen's life was inspired by his father's fascination with the military and by his own love for horses. "Even today," he says, laughing, "to sketch people I need models, but horses I can draw from memory!" When World War I broke out, he was one of the first officers to be commissioned in Poland's Lancer Regiment. The first year of the war saw the world's last cavalry campaigns, but De Rosen still remembers being knocked from his horse, unable to rise because of the weight of his armor. After the conflict ended, he returned to serious painting, refreshing his technique by taking courses at a school next to the Foreign Office, where he worked to support himself. De Rosen describes the next few years, during which he quietly refined his skills as an artist,

*A miniature manikin named Winifred, the lifelong companion of Jan De Rosen.*

as the most peaceful and satisfying of his life. When he wasn't working, he spent his time painting at one of the secluded country homes outside of Warsaw. "It was very exciting, there were no distractions, and I wasn't bothered by anyone but the flies."

Except for a brief interlude as a member of the Polish Delegation to the League of Nations, De Rosen spent every available moment at the easel. He finally had an opportunity to exhibit several of his works in

Warsaw. The show was a great success, and his reputation as a painter "took off like fireworks." Soon thereafter De Rosen was commissioned to create his first full-size mural. "Of course," he told me, "up until then I had had no walls to paint on, so all of my paintings were miniatures–about four feet by four feet." The transition from "miniatures" to a full-scale mural was no easy task, and by then, De Rosen remembers, "there was no one to tell me how to begin. I spent the first several weeks just staring at the huge blank walls." It took him five years to complete the mural, but by the time he finished, his talents were widely recognized. Other commissions and teaching positions followed. Then in 1937, at the request of the Polish ambassador, he traveled to the United States and the National Cathedral.

De Rosen's mural in the Chapel of St. Joseph of Arimathea, except for a slight mellowing of the tones, is as fresh today as when the colors were first applied decades ago–and it will remain a magnificent tribute, representative of the great tradition of encaustic muralists, for tens of decades to come.

# JEWELS OF THE CHAPEL

It ought to sparkle like a jewel box, in which the chamber is made of jewels and you're the little creature that walks within it. It should so surround you with sparkle and glitter that you wouldn't think about the concept of Resurrection, you would feel it." This was what he had in mind, Rowan LeCompte told me, when he designed his mosaics for the Cathedral's Resurrection Chapel. Located beneath the south transept, able to be reached only by means of a trek through the labyrinthine passageways of the crypt, it is easy, when you arrive in the chapel, to forget you are in the twentieth century. The architects tailored the room to be filled with a "spirited, colorful splendor," selecting a peaceful Norman theme that would harmonize architecturally with the vibrant covering of the walls and ceiling. Rowan LeCompte remembers Philip Frohman saying that what he hoped for was "colorful and figurative panels, separated by surfaces of stone." His intention, recalls LeCompte, was that "everything not stone should be either mosaic or mural." When the chapel is completed, only columns and carvings will be left of the bare stone; all the flat surfaces will sparkle with mosaics. The light-gray Indiana limestone adds to the natural coolness of the subterranean atmosphere. It is a perfect setting for walls of jewels.

Today there are seven murals in Resurrection Chapel; the principal one is the work of Hildreth Meiere of New York. The other six line the north and west walls and were designed by Rowan LeCompte, five of them in collaboration with his wife, Irene. Before the sixth mosaic could be completed, Irene LeCompte died, and it was decided to dedicate it to her memory.

Initially, the Cathedral's architects considered whether covering the walls with murals, instead of mosaics, might not be just as effective. So for years the chapel stood unembellished, handsomely Norman but without any of the artistic or spirited fervor Frohman had planned. In 1928 Frohman's partner, Donald Robb, traveled to Europe "to see the best examples of mural decoration in mosaic and fresco, and to compare the merits of each medium." Upon his return he wrote: "I first visited Sicily and saw there the three great examples of mosaic work, perhaps the greatest in the world, at Monreale, Cefalù, and in the Capella Palatina at Palermo. Later I inspected the earlier work at Ravenna and found some of a still earlier period in Rome. Of course, I saw also the mosaics in St. Mark's, Venice.

"In the work of the fresco painters I examined with care the decoration by Giotto, Cimabue, and Lorenzetti in Assisi; the beautiful series by Fra Angelico in San Marco, Florence, the excellent but slightly sophisticated work of Perugino in Perugia, Florence, and elsewhere. . . .

"For an effect of splendor . . . mosaic as a medium is without a rival. In this sense, the Capella Palatina is the finest interior I know. It is splendid in a quiet and reposeful way. Its coloring is rich without being bright, strong without being obtrusive; and in this respect it is unlike the modern mosaic which I have seen."

The Committee continued to deliberate, but the question answered itself when funds were donated for a mosaic in honor of William F. Draper, a general in the Union Army during the Civil War. The completed mosaic spreads across the half dome above the chapel altar. With almost mural-like realism and depth, lifelike figures depict the Resurrection against the background of a radiantly rising sun. The mosaic beneath the chancel arch predisposed the rest of the wall space decoration toward additional mosaics. Mixing media from wall space to wall space would have diminished the Gothic unity of the room.

The mosaic by Meiere is of the type described as marble or "stone" and was designed more than thirty years ago. Meiere has since died. I talked about her recently with Americo Bertoli, whose Venetian Art Mosaics company installed her mural in the Cathedral. Bertoli's company was once a booming atelier for mosaic artistry. Times have since changed. "I am the last of the line of her era of craftsmanship. I don't know of anyone who is left; they have all died."

Down the aisle from Meiere's peaceful mosaic of Christ Risen, the LeCompte tiles gleam panel after panel of figures surrounded by borders of asymmetric patterns—panels that are vibrantly alive depict Christ's reappearance. Until Rowan and Irene LeCompte were chosen to create these mosaics, Rowan LeCompte's creative expression had been almost wholly confied to stained glass, but in common with many other stained-glass artists, he seems equally at home in both media.

The narrow Norman chamber had captured LeCompte's imagination when he first saw it. As an artist in light, he had often wondered how he would solve the problem of decorating an underground chapel. "Because there is no daylight," he explained to me, "the room has a visual strike against it.

Though the design of the space is extremely impressive, without artificial light the place would be useless. The trick is for the embellishment to compensate for the monotone illumination."

Although he had had only limited experience in the medium, when LeCompte heard that the Cathedral's Building Committee was looking for an artist to design mosaics for the chapel, he submitted some of his and Irene's ideas to the Clerk of the Works. After they won the Building Committee's nod, the LeComptes spent a year in Istanbul studying the old Byzantine masters before deciding how to proceed.

When they returned, the LeComptes selected shiny "glass" mosaic tile for their design instead of the more muted "stone" tiles of the Meiere mosaic because, says LeCompte, "we were swayed toward the greater luster of porcelain by Frohman's request for 'colorful splendor.' The tempered tone and quality of stone mosaics might have been better if the rest of the walls and the ceiling were to remain quietly bare. But if the chapel is to be completed as a 'jewel box,' then it needs the glamour of glass–it needs to snap, crackle, and blaze like a huge bonfire; it should absolutely knock you off your feet."

Years after working with Hildreth Meiere, Americo Bertoli returned to the Cathedral to assist the LeComptes with installation of their designs. A master craftsman who had installed possibly more mosaics than any other artisan this side of the Atlantic, Bertoli has equal esteem for both enamel and marble. "Either material," he says, "it doesn't make much difference–both are extremely difficult to work with." Bertoli, who learned his craft in Florence, believes that to create a mosaic requires "a total understanding of the craft; one must be both a painter and a colorist, with the courage of a muralist and a compassion for tile."

It took several years for the six panels to

be completed. Just to install a mosaic is a lengthy and painstaking process. First, a life-size reproduction of the original design must be transferred in all its detail to heavy paper, the exact position of each of thousands of chips identified by shape and color. The paper is then covered with a wash of water-soluble glue, and, one by one, the tiles are hand-cut and placed face down on the pattern. When this is done, the tiled paper is cut into sections and the tiles are embedded section by section into the wet, cement-coated wall. The cement hardens, the paper is washed off, and the tiles are polished.

The mosaics of Resurrection Chapel are as permanent and enduring as the Cathedral itself. Mosaics of Byzantine and early Christian periods have come down through the centuries in better condition than virtually any other form of art. On his trip to Italy Robb noted that mosaics "undoubtedly have a great advantage over every form of painting. Nowhere could I discover any damage to mosaic from any cause save violence, and, as far as I could tell, the coloring is still as it was originally. The mosaics in Sicily, as you know, date from the twelfth century, the best of those in St. Mark's from the same, while the Ravenna work was done in the fifth and sixth and the apse of Santa Pudenziana in Rome is as early as the fourth. It is safe to assume that colors and workmanship which have stood sixteen hundred years will last indefinitely...." Not only are the materials extremely durable, but should there be any slight flaw or accidental damage, the individual tiles can be easily replaced. One thousand years from now the tiles of the chapel will be as arrestingly descriptive and as beautiful as they are today.

# A TREASURY
# OF NEEDLEWORK

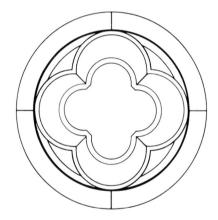

No one knows when the first needle was made–probably from bone–but it is certain that it took place in the dawn of civilization. And it is likely that shortly after plain sewing was invented, needles were also used to embroider primitive clothing. Every civilization has given birth to a textile tradition. And present-day Stone Age societies–like those who live in the jungles of Brazil–practice textile arts, even though they have yet to learn how to make pottery.

In Europe during the medieval period, sophisticated textile crafts burgeoned. Arabic influences, which had invaded Spain in the seventh century, slowly filtered across the Pyrenees, spreading word of new dyes and materials. The rising merchant class took advantage of the demand for these new products, and importing textiles became a profitable business; silk from China, wools from Persia, mohair from Angora–all were as eagerly awaited as the spices. Returning Crusaders introduced elaborate rugs from the east, which quickly found a market in the drafty Romanesque churches and castles, with their stone floors and unglazed windows.

In the great Gothic cathedrals enormous wall hangings served as portable partitions, dividing up vast spaces into areas for specific uses. Carpets bedecked the altars; banners flew in the heights of the hallways; frontals and other needlework added an array of bright colors to the chapels and chambers. The illustrative designs were rich and boundlessly elaborate, often portraying events in history of stories from the Bible. Sometimes the themes were taken from contemporary life because the textile craftsmen, like the carvers who work in stone, added their own ideas to their commissions. Much of the needlework was done by the women from the cathedral towns. For them plain sewing was a daily chore, but embroidery was the decorative use of their skill, a noble contribution to their cathedral. These women would have been surprised to hear themselves referred to as craftsmen, but so, nonetheless, they were, and many were supremely talented. For these medieval housewives, needlework was the only outlet for their creativity. As a result of their labors, cathedrals, abbeys, and even the parish houses of Europe were and still are decorated with beautiful textiles and needlepoint–from the magnificent tapestry of Flanders to the needlepoint and clerical vestments of England.

Europeans who came to America were, however, slow to extend their textile traditions to the new land, a frontier, and some three thousand miles by sea from tools and materials. Settlers had, of necessity, a simple life-style, and a needle and thread were prized possessions, used mainly for the basic needs of the home. But the art of needlework was not entirely neglected. Needlework samplers on which stitches were learned and practiced have been preserved as heirlooms, and passed on from generation to generation since the early days of the Colonies.

Gradually, as the wilderness was conquered and leisure time increased, decorative needlework began to develop in America. Old World and native American Indian techniques combined to enrich each other–as with the introduction of aniline dyes to the blanket-weaving tribes like the Navaho. By 1810 in New England there was a spinning wheel for every three people, quilting bees met nightly, and boys as well as girls grew up learning textile crafts as they assisted with household duties. But it was not until well into the nineteenth century that needlecraftsmen began to work outside of the home, and it was another century before textile crafts came into their own in America.

Of all the crafts represented in the National Cathedral, none has been worked by so many hands as the decorative stitchery. Construction had already been under way for fifty years when Francis Sayre became dean and, upon returning from a tour of European churches, suggested that textiles were the one craft missing from the Cathedral's Gothic embellishments. Building was well enough along, he felt, for the finishing touches to be added. "When walls and spires and lofty valuting are all in place, then must come that exquisite attention to small detail that prepares a cathedral's usefulness–colorful kneelers, cushions, rugs, and tapestries, when installed throughout the Cathedral will add warmth and love to the grey coldness of the bare stone."

Dean Sayre's proposal was greeted enthusiastically by some of the nation's most renowned women, who offered to lead a drive to fill the Cathedral with needlepoint embroidery. Sayre was delighted, and in June of 1954 he appointed Mrs. Harold Talbott, the wife of the Secretary of the Air Force, along with Mrs. George M. Humphrey, whose husband was then Secretary of the Treasury, and Mrs. Kevin Keegan, to found a Needlepoint Committee which would discover and organize needlecraftsmen who could create works for the Cathedral that were both "useful and decorative."

The three ladies immediately stirred up interest in the project. Assisted by many who were experienced in the craft, including Mrs. Theodore Roosevelt, they won support throughout the country by setting up a traveling exhibition of fine needlework. After an opening show at the Cathedral, the collection was shown in major cities, where it resulted in much publicity, for both needlepoint and the Cathedral. Contributions to the display came not only from professional craftsmen but from proficient amateurs as well. Actress Mary Martin loaned a large piece of expertly worked needlepoint which she herself had stitched backstage, and former United States Ambassador to Italy Clare Booth Luce loaned one of her favorite works. In all, more than one hundred of America's needlepoint craftsmen were represented.

When the Needlepoint Committee was formed, in 1955, the Cathedral did not yet have a nave, so the Committee concentrated its efforts on the eight chapels, the choir, and the high altar. Because the chapels are of different shapes and sizes, each with specially designed lighting, the Needlepoint Committee decided that all rugs, wall hangings, and cushions would have to be custom-made for each location. "In addition, all needlework for the Cathedral has special requirements," the present chairman, Mrs. Philip A. Rollings, told me. "Our needlework is really upholstery; it gets a great deal of wear, so it has to be exceptionally sturdy–and we expect it to last a century or more. For these reasons we use only the best materials. We use Persian wools throughout–a 3-ply yarn specially developed for mending Oriental rugs. When we started, it was the only wool available that came in a full color range; also the plies can be easily separated so it is ideal for 14-mesh canvas and for blending colors. Another thing is that we insist on oil paint for the painted canvases–no acrylics, because we don't know yet what acrylics do to fibers. Again, because we are planning for one hundred years, we don't take any chances."

Acting on advice from members of the Building Committee, the needlepointers decided it would be best to seek professional textile artists to design the patterns. "We felt that only experts had enough understanding of needlework—it is a medium with very specific problems—to tackle designs that would be compatible with the complex Gothic surrounds," explained Mrs. Helen Fredlund, who works closely with Mrs. Rollings. "The problem, however, was that experienced designers of needlework were not then on every corner as they are today. At that time just finding suitable materials and the right colors was difficult."

But the Needlepoint Committee tackled the problem ingeniously. In order to attract the greatest number of artists, and to gather them together in a situation where their work could be compared for quality and suitability, the committee organized a competition for needlepoint professionals. The contest was held concurrently with the needlepoint exhibition. Dean Sayre and Canon Monks, Mrs. Talbott and Mrs. Charles Hooks served as the judges, selecting the award winners and at the same time naming the designers who would be asked to submit their ideas for needlework in the Cathedral chapels. Mrs. Roosevelt, because of her great expertise, took charge of supervising the professionals who were commissioned.

The response to the traveling exhibition was enormous. From every state amateur needlecraftsmen volunteered to stitch the Cathedral's designs once they were completed. By October of 1955 the Needlepoint Committee reported it had formed regional groups of needleworkers, not only throughout this country but in England and France as well. The committee examined samples of needlepoint from hundreds of interested craftsmen and chose the most skillful ones to stitch the final designs.

Between 1954 and 1966 more than a thousand pieces of needlepoint were completed and put in place in the Cathedral. During that time more than twelve hundred artists, designers, and needleworkers participated in the project; they included craftsmen from the British West Indies, Colombia, Italy, and Norway, from England and France, and from every American state from Maine to Hawaii and Alaska.

Since the resignation of Mrs. Talbott, there have been a series of four equally able and energetic chairpersons. In 1957 Mrs. George Garrett took over leadership of the committee for two of its most frenetic years. Then in 1959 Mrs. Peter B. Freylinghuysen became chairperson for a year, followed by Mrs. Houghton Metcalf for a seven-year period, during which she supervised the assignment and working of several of the Cathedral's most important pieces, including the large wall hanging for the War Memorial Chapel. The present chairperson is Mrs. Philip A. Rollings, who was appointed by Dean Sayre in 1970. Mrs. Rollings has had a lifelong interest in needlework since she graduated from the University of California at Berkeley with a degree in the decorative arts.

Today there are only a few pieces of needlepoint that remain to be done. Except for any restoration of works in place, the committee's job is just about finished. "The only real possibility for new pieces," says Mrs. Rollings, "would be if someone should donate a new chair or communion rail or something of that sort; in that event the committee would commission needlepoint for it. We are doing a cushion for the stone benches in the west entrance and a nine-foot piece for a seat outside one of the crypts." In addition, Mrs. Rollings is presently in the third year of work on needlepoint for one of the sedilia seats on the south side of the high altar. She hopes to finish it by Christmas, but it is slow-going because she can work on it only during the daytime when the light is true enough for her to be able to "read" the fine shading of colors. The sedilia is a memorial to Robert Seibert, who did all of the Cathedral's upholstering until his tragic death at his shop, where he was trapped in a fire while trying to save the needlepoint he was working on.

In needlepoint embroidery not only does every stitch count, but each stitch must actually be counted into position, as though the interstices in the canvas are squares on graph paper. A single stitch out of place can spoil an entire design, so the process of filling in a design with colored wool is slow and laborious. It may take a designer as much as two months just to paint the design on an eighteen-inch-square canvas, and the stitching can easily take six times as long.

Mili Holmes of New Canaan, Connecticut, has designed more than seventy-five pieces of needlepoint for the Cathedral. Though she began as a professional textile designer when she was nineteen, she has designed everything from Schumacher wallpaper to lampshades. "I love working on the Cathedral," she told me, "much more than on any of my other projects because it is going to be there for a long, long while, and also because it will be used so much more importantly."

"Needlepoint," said Mili Holmes, "is one of the last of the textile arts that I seriously considered. I left Grand Central Arts School in New York City when I was still in my teens to work as an industrial designer. That was when I learned never to make a mistake–everything was mass-produced and if, for example, I designed a wallpaper pattern that was off by an eighth of an inch, an entire lot would come out wrong. I learned to be very careful and did well in the business. When I started having children, I went into free-lancing, but by then most of my work was too highly styled for regular commercial purchase. I actually started doing needlepoint out of personal interest. Because of my designer background I naturally painted my own canvases. Someone saw me stitching one and asked me to make them a canvas,

then more and more people started sending me requests, and I found myself in the needlepoint trade.

"I like designing needlepoint because I can talk personally with the individuals who are going to live with it–I like having the opportunity to work on a piece until it is right. I always have said, 'Never mind what someone else has done; just do what you want to do, but do it right!'"

Mili Holmes became involved with the Cathedral's needlepoint through the Tebbetts sisters. The four sisters, who designed the rug at the Cathedral's high altar, were among the earliest needlepoint designers in America, running a studio in Lyme, Connecticut. One day, "out of the blue," Mary Tebbetts (who is still stitching at the age of one hundred) telephoned Mili Holmes. "We had never met or even talked before, but Miss Tebbetts said she and her sisters were getting ready to retire and she said they had seen my work and they wanted me to take over their work. Shortly after that the Cathedral asked me to submit some sketches and..."

Mrs. Holmes's cushions for St. Mary's Chapel and her communion-rail kneelers for Bethlehem Chapel have drawn much praise and have won her commissions from many great American churches and places of worship, including the chapel of Groton School, which Henry Vaughan designed before being named Cathedral architect. Standing in her studio surrounded by counters covered with samples of wool–a giant palette of over three hundred colors–Mili Holmes showed me details of her workmanship: precisely formed Chinese characters, calligraphy that she not only painted on the canvas but carefully stitched herself to assure a perfect Taiwan seal in petit point on a choir cushion for the Cathedral. "When I first went to work for the Cathedral, people had never heard of needlepoint–they thought I was out of my mind when I talked about the sort of artist I am. Now needlepoint canvases are being mass-produced, but the Cathedral and I are still doing things the old way–we still insist on individual handwork."

Once the artist finishes painting a design on the canvas, the canvas is passed on to a craftsman for stitching. Most of the craftsmen used by the Cathedral are skilled amateurs who either have other professions or are housewives. "A major reason it is so great to design for the Cathedral," Mili Holmes said, "is because I know that what I design will be properly stitched–to work for the Cathedral, a stitcher must first pass close scrutiny by the committee. They are asked to send in some of their work and it is carefully examined–on both sides, because the back is as important as the front." Mrs. Rollings subsequently described the nature of the test to me. "Each prospective needleworker must submit a two-inch-square sample of their basket weave, worked on 14-mesh canvas. We receive many applications, but only a few of the finest are selected."

The French unbleached canvas used at the Cathedral is usually single-thread mono-weave; occasionally, however, a double-thread canvas is chosen so that both needle-point and the much finer petit point can be worked on the same canvas. The diagonal tent stitch is standard for most patterns because it stands up well to wear and retains its blocked shape. However, other stitches, such as the Gobelin, Scotch, and diagonal Cash-mere, may also be found in some of the chapels. One of the altar frontals for St. Mary's Chapel is decorated with couching–the tacking of gold and silver thread into the design.

Though the layman might assume that the person who fills in the designer's painted canvas with colored yarn is simply following instructions and has no creative contribution

*A giant palette of wool spread before her, Mili Holmes combs a cardinal skein.*

to make to the piece, this is far from the case. Like the carvers who transfer a sculptor's plaster into stone, the stitcher makes many decisions that determine whether a piece will work. For example, it is often left for the needleworker to select one shade of color over another, or to choose the technique for blending two colors; these fine decisions, combined with the quality of the handiwork, can make all the difference in the appearance of the finished design.

The larger works of needlepoint at the Cathedral were stitched in sections by groups of craftsmen. The rug that was designed by the Tebbetts sisters for the high altar was given out to be stitched, after taking the sisters a year to prepare the canvas, in

105

twenty-two separate pieces. Twenty-two women from Pittsburgh, Pennsylvania, spent the next twelve months completing the stitching. When all of the pieces were finished, they were carefully sewn together with hidden seams–composing the nine-by-twenty-one-foot rug. Had the rug been made by a single craftsman, it would have taken twenty years.

In the War Memorial Chapel there is a wood-framed needlepoint wall-hanging ten feet wide and twelve feet tall. A memorial to Americans who died in war, the design is based on the biblical tree of Jesse, with limbs supporting the seals of all fifty states. Each seal is a foot in diameter and was worked on a separate canvas which was then appliquéd onto the tree. The Bryn Mawr studio of Mrs. Henry Earnshaw spent two and a half years readying the design. Artist Dorothy Hutton used oil-base colors to outline the tree and its vined border on the large canvas. And eighty-nine American women did the needlework.

The kneelers that hang from the backs of the chairs in the War Memorial Chapel are especially interesting. They were all stitched by English craftsmen, led by Lady Reading, a member of Parliament who organized the British project as a gift of thanks for America's assistance to Great Britain during World War II. One of the geometric designs is the work of Elizabeth, the Queen Mother. "The kneelers are among our finest," Mrs. Rollings told me. "The English have specialized in needlepoint for centuries and are very advanced. They nearly always work from charts, counting out the stitches onto the canvas, rather than using the painted canvases we tend to have in this country."

In return for the gift from England, nine members of the Cathedral Needlepoint Committee stitched forty-two feet of needlepoint which was given to Canterbury Cathedral for use as kneelers at their altar. One worker alone contributed more than half a million stitches to the design, which incorporates the official flower of every state in the Union.

St. John's Chapel tells the history of the United States through needlepoint kneelers that portray the lives of 175 famous American men and women drawn from a list specially compiled by a group of historians at the Smithsonian Institution. Depicted by a kneeler with a "V for victory" hand sign and the British lion rampant, Winston Churchill, honored by Congress with American citizenship, is represented among other famous Americans.

On either side of the slype, where the clergy is robed, cushions are decorated with stylized renderings of the Cathedral staff. Down in the crypt chapel of St. Joseph of Arimathea the kneelers are embroidered with a design that includes hyssop, aloes, and myrrh, the biblical burial herbs.

Without banners no Gothic cathedral would be complete. Dean Sayre accordingly suggested that flags and banners be added. Eventually official state flags were donated from each of the fifty states; they hang in the north and south transepts. Other areas that have afforded an opportunity for beautiful needlework are the richly embroidered vestments and frontals, which change with the services.

Artist Marjorie Coffey's first work for the Cathedral was a banner for the Rare Book Room. A professional who began her career as a sculptor and painter, and later achieved international recognition for her jewelry designs, Coffey enjoys working with textiles more than any other medium. "Working with fabrics is the culmination of everything I have ever done, from the crocheting and quilting I did for my grandmother long ago, to my work as a designer and colorist. For me, fabrics are alive–shifting gracefully as they move with the wearer, rippling as they are stirred by a breeze...."

After making a second banner for the Cathedral, a modern design–ten feet tall–that incorporates pieces of bright blue and orange vinyl, Coffey submitted an idea she had for vestments. It was in 1974, just as the Cathedral was making arrangements for the installation of John Maury Allin as Presiding Bishop of the Episcopal Church. Her sketches were so well received that she was asked to make vestments for the ceremony. Vestments, Coffey feels, are a difficult design problem. "If a vestment is distracting, it is wrong; it must enhance without disrupting. The liturgy is a drama, but it must be handled with reverence–it is not just to entertain an audience. Vestments have to be tailored, not only to the surroundings, but to the person who wears it. A vestment is a banner that moves; it's all choreography–a design that looks well on the wall won't necessarily move well on a person. Vestments are as individual as the people they are made for—I like to have them involved, to get to know the wearer."

Once Coffey had roughed out her design for the Cathedral's vestments, her next task was the selection of exactly the right material. "I need to know that the material will feel right; for instance, if it is too heavy, it will never be comfortable. It is important that it flows with the person's movements. No two people are the same and the right material for one can be very wrong for another. I hunted and hunted for the right fabric for Bishop Allin, and finally sent to New York City for a hard-finished silk and wool worsted. I bought all the material they had–it was just enough to make the three vestments and miters; there was no more available anywhere. It was the most expensive fabric I had ever worked with. I was very apprehensive, but it turned out to be beautiful to work with–with enough body so it would stand out from the wearer."

In keeping with Bishop Allin's wish that his installment symbolize equality, he requested that all the miters be made the same height and all white, without colorful decoration. Yet Coffey still managed to lend the miters a touch of elegance by embroidering them in white. "To create lines of light and shadow I combined silk cord with some wool and some cotton and even some mohair. The textured decoration was effective, even at a distance."

For Coffey, her work is her favorite way of spending her time. "My art is my life and my work is my recreation. I have worked for museums and all sorts of places, but until I began making ecclesiastical textiles for the Cathedral, there was never any of the personal quality, of my designs being worn and really used. The Cathedral has all the excitement and pageantry of the theater, but is on a serious and meaningful level for the enhancement of something beyond man."

# MUSIC ON THE CLOSE

No one notices the two men stride across St. John's Chapel and disappear through the small wooden doorway, nearly hidden in the pattern of the south choir wall. But a few moments later, slowly and deliberately, the Great Organ begins to play and a soloist's sturdy voice rolls down the aisle. Visitors are scattered throughout the nave. Now they stop and stand in wonder, surprised by this supreme touch of the Gothic hand.

One day, work on the stone and wood carving will come to an end; the stained glass will all be installed. The Cathedral will at last be completed and the crews of stonemasons and other craftsmen will be dispersed forever–but the musicians and the music will remain. Bells will ring and organs will resound; men and boys will sing in the choir. For music is the living soul of the Cathedral. Far more than just an artistic expression, music at the Cathedral is the realization of the dream that motivated the Cathedral's founders and that spurred on the Cathedral's vast army of builders. This was their goal: a structure that would be a singing statement of praise to God, transcending the times in which it was constructed and serving the entire country as a symbol of morality and national conscience.

Cathedral music evolved from choral chants, born in the Middle East long before Rome. After the thirteenth century, organs and sometimes one or two additional instruments began to accompany the choirs; these are the roots of Western classical music. It was in the churches, particularly the great churches of Europe, that this music was nurtured to maturity. Mozart, Scarlatti, Bach,

and Handel, all contributed to this rich legacy. Today the music program of the National Cathedral spans the centuries since the first choir, yet it also looks to the future, committed to the presentation of new music and new idioms, mixing innovative and avant-garde with the more familiar traditional.

Music was in the minds of the Cathedral's planners from the very beginning. The Cathedral's primary architect, Philip Hubert Frohman, designed the shape of the nave to be as kind as possible to sound–no simple task, since the aesthetic and structural requirements of Gothic architecture are not generally conducive to good acoustics. Frohman, an amateur musician himself, was careful to select building materials that would cause the least dissonance and interference in the sound of the organ and choir. The story is told that at one point he had already begun lining a section of the nave with a special type of tile when some of the musicians informed him that this material would tend to deaden sound. Frohman responded immediately and switched to a more congenial material. His design for the nave, when compared to virtually any of the world's great Gothic churches and especially when compared to other contemporary churches, is an acoustical masterpiece. The total "decay" of reverberation, even on the lowest tremolos of the full organ, is less than six seconds. Though this is too much echo for some types of music, the total elimination of reverberation was not Frohman's intent. What he sought, and to a very great extent achieved, was control of the notes bouncing off the architectural elements of the nave, for some degree of reverberation is desirable in most church music. A listener sitting in the rear of the nave may not hear a running passage in an allegro chorus of Handel's *Messiah* as crisply as in the Kennedy Center for the Performing Arts. On the other hand, no concert hall allows those marvelously joyous hallelujahs to come marching so triumphantly back.

The careful attention paid to acoustics enables the Cathedral to host a wide variety of music with success. Certainly, for a Gothic structure it is exceptionally versatile.

Ever since the Cathedral has had roof enough to protect instruments from the weather, music has been played atop Mount St. Alban. In 1912 a choir was formed, and while the personnel has turned over many times, the choir has continued without interruption to the present day. St. Albans Cathedral School was actually established to provide an education for the twenty-six young boys who, joined with twenty-two men, form the Cathedral choir. The boys usually begin singing when they are seven or eight years old. They rehearse and perform upwards of fifteen hours a week until, at about fourteen years of age, their voices change. Unlike many of the other great church choirs, the choir of the National Cathedral travels rarely, primarily because it is truly a working choir responsible throughout the year for several services a week.

Composed of serious singers, responsible for a large and varied repertory, the choir takes pride in the fact that it does not repeat the same works over and over during the year. In a single recent twelve-month period the choir learned and performed over 530 hymns and psalms, 218 anthems, and more than 150 settings and canticles.

As the building of the Cathedral progressed, enlargement of the nave made it possible to accommodate a considerably larger audience, and beginning in the early sixties a comprehensive plan was set in motion to expand the music program. The Great Organ was rebuilt and enlarged, and both a ten-bell ring and a fifty-three-bell carillon were installed in the Gloria in Excelsis Tower. Dr. Paul Callaway, who had joined the staff and become organist and choirmaster just prior to World War II, laid the groundwork for a College for Church Musicians, and in 1965 he was largely instrumental in initiating a summer concert program. Because of Dean Sayre's interest and enthusiastic support, funds were drawn from the daily budget to implement the program.

Although the completion of construction remained the primary fiscal priority, the fact that operating funds were allocated toward an expanded music program speaks for the Cathedral's desire to be a true, everyday working church–not merely a memorial to a bygone era. As with its construction, the Cathedral financed its music without any assistance or grant from either government or organized church.

In developing the concept for a College of Church Musicians, Callaway worked closely with Richard Wayne Dirksen, then precentor of the Cathedral. In 1962 at the invitation of the Cathedral, Leo Sowerby, internationally known as a composer of both church and secular music, left his teaching post at the American Conservatory of Music in Chicago to come to Washington and head the new institute. Sowerby, who had been awarded a Pulitzer Prize for his *Canticle of the Sun*, brought his personal prestige to the new college and helped to gain for it instant recognition. To assure one-to-one instruction, the first year's class was limited to a total of just six students, nor was the enrollment ever allowed to exceed fifteen new students a year. Admission was based on an applicant's "avocation in church music"; although many of those accepted were college graduates, no prior education was specifically required. During its brief existence (1962–69) the College of Church Musicians was the only such school in the United States attached to a

(Above) *The National Cathedral from the southwest. The Linden crane reaches across the unfinished west end. When completed, two towers will rise 234 feet on either side of the west facade.* (Right) *The facade of the north transept and the Women's Porch.*

(Left) *Like a modern sculpture, the apse—winged with flying buttresses—reaches for the sky.*
(Below) *Sunrise above the north porch balcony on a hazy summer morning.*

*The Gloria in Excelsis Tower at night.*

(Above) *A spider web of vaulting washed in color by the windows above the choir.*
(Left) *The choir and the high altar from the crossing. The Canterbury pulpit is on the right.*

(Above) *The alabaster sepulcher of Henry Yates Satterlee, the first Bishop of Washington, rests in the quiet light of the apse of Bethlehem Chapel.* (Right) *The interior of the apse.*

*High altar reredos seen from the crossing.*
(Photo by Morton Broffman)

*A service in the crossing bordered
by the massive pillars
of the Gloria in Excelsis Tower.*

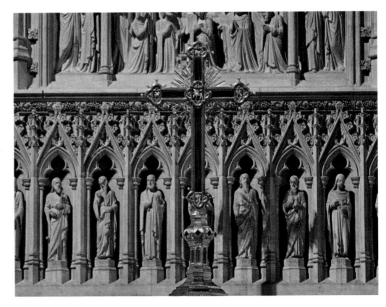

(Above) *Prophets of the Old
Testament carved in the
Caen stone of the high altar
reredos.* (Left) *A quatrefoil
in the west balcony frames
the nave.*

*A mosaic of marble paves the choir—green from
quarries of Maryland, pink and
brown from Tennessee, wine-red from Vermont,
and gold from Italy.*

*The west rose from the choir with the vaulting of the nave golden in midday sunlight.*

(Above) *Throughout the day the stained-glass windows create an ever-changing light show in the Cathedral's interior. Above the balcony blooms the south rose.* (Above right) *Looking down the nave toward the central windows of the apse designed by Wilbur Burnham and Joseph Reynolds.*
(Right) *A nave window tells Brother Lawrence's story of a war-weary soldier who regains hope when he discovers "the withered trees will bloom again."*

*A prism precisely placed in Rowan LeCompte's west rose bursts into a series of rainbow colors at sunset as the light slowly fades into darkness.*

*Christ in Majesty, the center apse window, designed by Burnham and Reynolds.*

(Above) *Stars sparkle and constellations wheel in Rodney Winfield's Space Window. Near the top of the center lancet is a moon rock given to the Cathedral by the crew of* Apollo XI. (Right) *Lawrence Saint's north rose window is a colorist's delight—the culmination of a lifetime devoted to the discovery of medieval stained-glass formulas.*

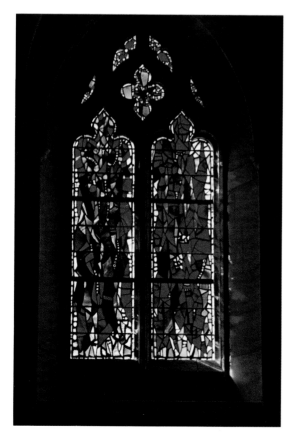

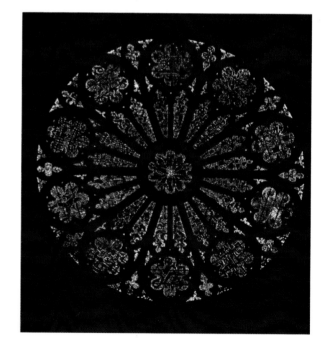

(Above) *''Creation,'' Rowan LeCompte's west rose window. Breaking with the tradition of pictorial design, the stained glass blazes with kinetic abstract patterns.* (Left) *A vibrant abstract design in stained glass, one of the* America the Beautiful *Windows.*

(Above) *An early indication of the skill of Jacob Schmidt: the Bishop, an apprentice piece, forms the handle on the slype door.*
(Right) *Leaving the Chapel of St. Joseph of Arimathea.*

*Holy Spirit Chapel is many people's favorite. The wrought-iron gates are the work of Samuel Yellin; the oak reredos frames a mural by N. C. Wyeth.*

(Right) *St. Joseph of Arimathea* (right) *in a detail from Jan De Rosen's mural. De Rosen used people at the Cathedral as his models.* (Below) *The mosaic by Hildreth Meiere fills the chancel arch of the crypt chapel of the Resurrection.*

*Frohman's vision of "spirited colorful splendor" is brought to life with this jewel-like mosaic by Rowan and Irene LeCompte in Resurrection Chapel.*

*A detail from one of the sixteenth-century Flemish tapestries that line the walls of the choir chapel of St. Mary.*

(Above) *St. George (left) and St. Michael slay dragons in the petit point centers of the two altar kneelers of War Memorial Chapel. English needlecraftsmen stitched all of the kneelers in the chapel as a gift of thanks for America's assistance during World War II. (Left) Oak leaves border the cushions of the carved choir stalls. The seal is that of the Episcopal Missionaries of the Virgin Islands.*

*Even the organ in the Children's Chapel is scaled down to accommodate the small visitor.*

working church. Each student received individual instruction and was encouraged to become involved in writing and performing modern music. In addition, he was required to play every week at actual services, after which he would go through a session of criticism with his instructor. The fact that the Cathedral has a large enough number of services to accommodate such a program (there are some sixteen hundred services a year) combined with excellent music facilities and an exceptional staff brought the college to immediate national attention as a unique school of music. During its seven years of operation it graduated some of the finest church musicians of our time. Nevertheless, in 1969, shortly after Sowerby's death, the college closed its doors.

In 1965 the Cathedral held the first in a series of summer music festivals. In July and August as many as sixteen events were offered free of charge to the public; ballet, plays, recitals, folk music, and jazz were performed both indoors and outdoors on the steps of the south transept. The summer program lasted ten years, until 1976, when lack of funds forced it to be discontinued. One of the program's goals was to encourage performers to present their very best work. "The building was itself a statement," says Wayne Dirksen, "against which anything they did had to be measured." In fact, the Cathedral insisted that performers be cognizant of the building as a unique stage, not just another concert hall or theater setting. A case in point is the story Wayne Dirksen tells of his repeated efforts to get José Limón, the great modern dancer and choreographer, to make an appearance at the Cathedral. Dirksen first phoned Limón's manager in New York. "She told me that the cost would be so-and-so and asked what date we wanted. I tried to explain," Dirksen recalls, "that before the Cathedral set up anything final, we wanted Limón to come and see the place." Several months elapsed and still nothing was

settled, though on two occasions when Limón was in Washington his manager phoned to set up a performance date. But the Cathedral insisted he come and see the setting first. Finally one day, "just about dark," says Dirksen, "Limón arrived. I met him and took him to the nave. When we reached the crossing, Limón came suddenly alive with enthusiasm and, leaping across the open space, struck a column with his palm. I thought I saw the column move and figured that anyone who could move one of those columns was meant to perform in the Cathedral!"

The College of Church Musicians closed, as we have said, in 1969, and the last summer festival took place in 1976. Paul Callaway, who recently received the Order of the British Empire, England's highest honor for a foreign citizen, has gone into active retirement. Dean Sayre has also retired. But the Cathedral's intense interest in music remains undiminished. Dr. Callaway told me he is looking forward to the day when the College of Church Musicians will reopen, this time "with an expanded course of instruction that will include dance and drama and eventually every other church art." And Wayne Dirksen, whose son Rick is now the Cathedral's master bell ringer, is confident that in time music on the close will again flourish as it did during the sixties and early seventies. Without a doubt music daily plays life into the great church. In the year 1976 alone sixty-five choral societies from all parts of the country sang in the Cathedral, and Wayne Dirksen, now the Cathedral organist and choirmaster, feels that this sort of participation is one of the essential, ongoing aspects of music on Mount St. Alban. "When you add up the total number of musicians and singers and actors who have performed here, it runs into the thousands. They are all part of the music at the Cathedral–performing here is itself a valuable, subjective experience for each of the musicians."

113

# 10,000 PIPES

*The organ, to my eyes and ears, is the king of instruments.*
W. A. Mozart, letter to his father, October 17, 1777.

Slowly the Great Organ begins to play. The rich, sonorous chords and powerful harmonies flow into the nave, filling every corner with waves of sound. Only the architectural lines that lead toward the high altar offer a clue as to the music's source, for it seems to emanate from the very limestone itself.

Organs were relative latecomers to Gothic architecture. Though the *organum hydraulicum* had been invented by Ctesibius of Alexandria 250 years before the birth of Christ, the art of building organs had been lost, and was not rediscovered until the ninth century, when very simple organs of the clavichord and harpsichord type began to be used in Christian churches. The first chromatic organ did not appear until the fourteenth century–midway into the Gothic era. While it was one of the last of the embellishments to be added to the great churches of the period, the organ was so apt an accompaniment to the other Gothic arts that today it is difficult for us to imagine a Gothic church without one, so integral a part of every Gothic church does it seem to be.

Just as the great cathedral builders of the Middle Ages could not have foreseen the intricate musical instruments that would one day add a final grace note to their creation, those who first conceived of the National Cathedral never could have imagined the amount of technical knowledge and craftsmanship that would ultimately come together to design and construct the Cathedral's Great Organ many years later. Drawing their first plans at a time when the first record player was just beginning to appear and simple box cameras were just becoming available to the public, the founders of the National Cathedral never dreamed of a single organ with a nerve center of thousands of electrical circuits governing winds feeding thousands of pipes. Nonetheless, the Great Organ is as much at home in the National Cathedral as it would be if the Cathedral had been built around it. And, of course, when it is learned that Philip Hubert Frohman, the Cathedral's architect, was himself regarded as an authority on the design and voicing of organs, it is not outside the realm of possibility that it was!

Frohman was not only an enthusiast of organs and organ music, he often became involved in building the organs he designed. To this avocation he added a keen interest in electricity and how electricity could be applied to the operation of highly complex organs. One of Frohman's inventions was an organ with two keyboards, which he proceeded to install in the Cathedral. The versatility and convenience of having one console in the Children's Chapel and another in the north triforium gallery made his instrument a unique treat. One of the first remote-control organs, it could be played with equal ease from either location.

The Cathedral's first organ was installed in Bethlehem Chapel in 1912, only five years after the foundation stone was laid, but more than fifty years before the completion of the central tower. It was a four-manual instrument built by Ernest M. Skinner, one of the great innovators in twentieth-century organ design, and for twenty years it performed as the Cathedral's principal service instrument. In 1953 G. Donald Harrison, head of the now-

117

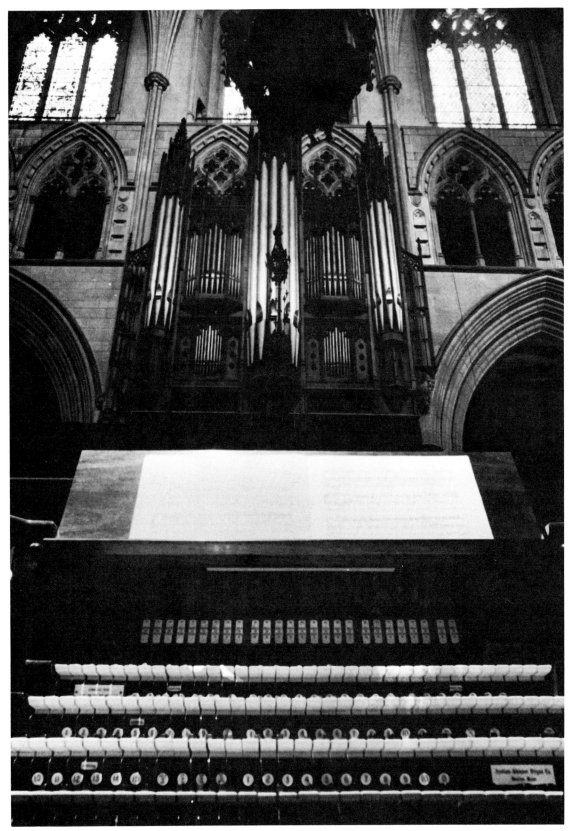

*The Great Organ.*
(Photo by Morton Broffman)

legendary Aeolian-Skinner Organ Company, was asked to design an electropneumatic organ to replace the original one now worn by use. This is the organ that may be heard in Bethlehem Chapel today.

The Cathedral's Great Organ, also designed by Ernest Skinner, was installed in 1937–38, when no south transept yet existed. The temporary ceiling over the crossing was only forty feet high, and there was no nave at all. Skinner was forced to tailor his design to what he could only estimate would be its effect in the completed chamber. For Skinner, it was the culmination of a rich and fruitful career spanning over forty years of work, the last of his many large installations. With a four-manual-and-pedal console, it had a total of over eight thousand pipes; it required literally miles of cable, two huge blowers in a crypt one hundred feet below, and an elaborate system of wind ducts leading up to the level of the nave and triforium. It was considered by Skinner to be his finest work.

It is noteworthy that Frohman took upon himself the task of designing the handsome Gothic panels that are incorporated in the oak casing that houses the console.

The Cathedral's Great Organ, unlike organs in most churches (which hold only three or four services a week), is played an average of six hours a day. By 1956 Skinner's use-worn console was in need of replacement. And it was decided that the leathers and contacts of the instrument needed a complete overhaul. As plans began to be drawn for a new keyboard, the committee appointed for the purpose by Dean Sayre began to consider revamping the organ piping as well. Clearly, if this were ever to be done, it would be best to plan pipes and console at the same time. The Cathedral had grown considerably since the organ's installation, and it was decided not only to take care of the immediate needs of the instrument but also to make plans for whatever alterations and additions the committee felt would be

needed to make the organ compatible with the spatial requirements of the finished Cathedral.

In 1957 Dr. Joseph Whiteford (who had succeeded Harrison as head of Aeolian-Skinner) was selected to put on paper plans for renovation of the entire instrument. In 1958 he built an enlarged console to match the plans and specifications he had drawn up, incorporating the Gothic panels Frohman had designed for the original console. Between 1963 and 1965, a six-stop brustwerk, a positiv, and a sixty-one-note trompette en chamade were added, but it was to be another twelve years before the pipes caught up to the potential of the new keyboard. Meanwhile, adhesive tape ascribed temporary tasks to many knobs which would one day be freed to serve the enlarged organ.

The console is the brain of an organ. Sound is created by wind forced through pipes–each designed to play a single note. Since the pressure of the wind sent to each pipe must be constant, the only way to increase the volume of a note is to have more than one pipe tuned to the same pitch.

Thus, in some large organs, such as the Cathedral's, as many as one hundred pipes are devoted to a single note. By selecting controls on the console, the organist determines how many pipes of a given pitch will play at one time. The console pedals, which are connected to reservoirs of air called swell boxes, are another means of varying volume. When opened, they supply an extra reserve of air, usually to an entire row of keys at the same time.

Unlike other keyboard instruments, most organs have two or more rows of keys. Each row is called a manual and is actually a complete instrument in itself. By manipulating several manuals at once, the organist is able to play polyphonic music in two or more contrasting parts. He can, for instance, highlight the melody, or principal parts, against a chordal accompaniment, at the same time

*The console of the Great Organ.*

trumpeting loud sections and playing quieter passages in quick succession. Additional sets of controls, called stops, enable the organist to sound specific, preselected ranks of pipes tuned to resemble the sound of other instruments, thereby creating special effects. For example, stop number 61 on the Cathedral's renovated Great Organ combines 68 pipes which create a sound imitating the English horn; stop 22 combines 128 pipes and is called the fourth gross kornett.

In 1971, with the drive to finish the nave by 1976, the nation's Bicentennial Year, Dean Sayre urged the completion of the Great Organ. The plans were all drawn, but they were extraordinarily elaborate. Then, too, the costs for materials and highly skilled craftsmen had increased greatly. Few large organs were being ordered and, as a result, Aeolian-Skinner and others in the field had gone bankrupt in the mid-sixties. It seemed un-

likely that any of the companies left would be either willing or able to adhere to the intricate 1957 plans. It was Wayne Dirksen's father who suggested to the Building Committee that they undertake to do the job themselves. And so the Cathedral Organ Consortium was formed. It brought together many of the last organ craftsmen in America. Dr. Joseph S. Whiteford, the designer who twenty years earlier had drawn up the plans, was persuaded to step out of retirement to supervise the organ's completion.

Renovation began in 1973. Dr. Whiteford worked closely with Roy Perry, an organ builder from Texas, with Robert Wyant, who had helped service the organ for years, and with Cathedral Organist Callaway. Wayne Dirksen served as coordinator for the Cathedral. The four-year project was to result in the addition of nearly two thousand pipes.

Work was begun with the same zeal for

120

*A forest of pipes—just a few of the more than ten thousand that belong to the Great Organ.*

*The low notes of the Great Organ come from pipes made of simple wooden planks.*

perfection that has marked every phase of building. The use of a tape recorder made it possible to make instant comparisons with the great organs in Europe. From the recordings they learned that the pipe pressures of the great Old World organs were much lower than they had thought. This discovery led to voicing that is extremely clear, with great beauty of tone.

When the renovation and enlargement of the Great Organ was finished, the organ was impressively close to Whiteford's original 1957 plans. It is one of the ironies of cathedral builders, who often take on endeavors too great for a single lifetime, that Dr. Whiteford, who now lives in California and is no longer willing to fly, has never heard the magnificent instrument that is so largely his own creation.

Completed in 1976, the organ is composed of 10,250 pipes ranging from high-pitched metal piccolo pipes the thickness of a finger to bombarde basse pipes sixty-four feet in length made of simple wooden planks. Hundreds of miles of wire connect the 180 ranks of pipes to the four-manual-and-pedal console, with 151 stops controling 115 voices, 472 contact relays, and over 10,000 electrical circuits. Huge ducts transport compressed air to the pipes from the blower room below the crypt, where large electric blowers re-place the hand-manned bellows of medieval times. So extraordinary is the power of the Great Organ's voice that a single key can drown out the combined resources of the Philadelphia and Boston orchestras.

Paul Callaway has given organ recitals all over the world, playing some of the finest instruments ever constructed. He says, however, that of all the great organs which he has played, "large, medium, and small, there is none more versatile than the Great Organ of the National Cathedral–and nowhere is there one so grand."

In addition to the Great Organ, there are two other organs in the Cathedral that are worthy of special mention.

The Organ in Resurrection Chapel is a duplexed, two-manual-and-pedal organ built by Skinner in 1939. It was originally installed in the Chapel of St. Joseph of Arimathea but is now to be found in Resurrection Chapel.

The Portativ, a portable organ designed and built by the Reuter Organ Company in 1962, is used to accompany smaller services or concerts. It is a flexible, compact instrument, complete with pipes, blower, and wind chests in a cherrywood case. Concealed rubber-tired wheels allow it to be moved without difficulty by three men.

# THE TOWER OF BELLS

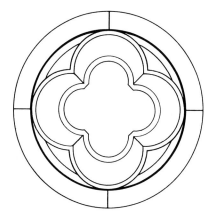

Together with drums, bells are among the most ancient of musical instruments. Bells of many shapes and sizes have been uncovered in archaeological excavations near Babylon and in pre-Colombian sites. Hammered from gold and silver, they sounded in China centuries before Confucius, and during the days of the Emperors rows of bells, lined up according to size, doubled as standard for weights or, turned upside down, to check the accuracy of measures. It is said that the first church bell in Europe was used in Italy in the town of Campania, during the fifth century, to summon villagers to religious services. During the next few hundred years the use of call bells spread northward and eastward throughout medieval Europe, and when villages became towns they also served as municipal alarms, warning of fire, attack, or other common danger. As life became increasingly complex, other bells were added, and instead of a single call bell, several bells were hung together. Every person in a town learned to associate the sound of a particular bell with the event it reported: gates open in the morning, gates secured at dusk, curfew (meaning "fires out," to reduce hazards during the night) and calls to action, such as "dikes burst." As more and more signals were needed, whatever bells were available were added to those already in the towers, many of which accumulated quite an assortment of sizes, shapes, and sounds.

Until the eighth century, bells were fashioned out of many different metals and dozens of different alloys: lead, iron, gold, silver, zinc, and tin. What revolutionized bellmaking was the discovery of bronze casting. The tin and copper alloy made it possible to have bells with the strength of copper and the clear tone of tin. For suprisingly enough, it is the tin that gives bells their "silvery" ring; silver itself, like most other metals, sounds dull and foggy. By the end of the Gothic period bells, which had ranged in form from long and narrow to quadrangular to miter-shaped, began to be made in the familiar cuplike form of bells today, and the quality and consistency of their tone was further improved.

By the early part of the sixteenth century, bells were beginning to be played as crude musical instruments. In Belgium and Holland, a system of weighted pendulums, the first "clock" mechanism, was rigged in bell towers to rotate large barrels fitted with protruding wooden pegs. As the barrels turned, the pegs struck the bells and routine signals of the day were sounded automatically. (The principle of the rotating barrel led to the invention of both the music box and the barrel organ.) With the addition of more pegs and more bells, instead of sounding individual notes, whole tunes could be played at regular intervals to mark the passage of the day. Eventually the more complex of these early clock towers played a tune every seven and a half minutes (eight times an hour) twenty-four hours a day. A major problem, however, was that changing the sequence in which the bells rang required several hours' work reordering the pegs. The ingenious solution was to do away with the pegs (which worked automatically once they were set in place) and substitute instead a manual key-

127

*Change bells yoked to swing almost soundlessly.*

board. Each key was now connected by wires to a hammer (or clapper) inside a bell. Striking a key pulled the clapper against the bell and sounded a tone. Thus the keyboard enabled a trained bell ringer to sit down and instantly play the appropriate tunes for the particular occasion. This was the advent of the carillon–born, contrary to the usual sequence of invention, regressing from automatic to manual.

At the same time that carillons were evolving in the Low Countries, across the North Sea the British also began playing more than one bell together. Although they, too, began by pulling the clapper against a stationary bell, the English discovered that by swinging the bell itself, centrifugal force would drive the clapper against the bell. This greatly increased the volume of sound and best utilized the shape of the bell. The mouth swinging first in one direction, then in the other, tossed the sound around, creating a Doppler effect which maximized the bell's tone. Swinging a bell that weighs several tons could not be accomplished from a manual keyboard, no matter how efficient its system of weights and balances. Instead, each bell was rung separately, not by means of a keyboard, but with a rope pulled by hand. A seventeenth-century printer named Fabian Stedman of Cambridge, England, is credited with being the father of change ringing, the continual production of bell ringing without repetition of the same sequence. He was the first to work out the various combinations, or changes, mathematically possible with six, seven, eight–up to a total of twelve bells.

Thus on the continent of Europe the

towers of the great churches rang with the carillon's graceful harmonies, and in the British Isles powerful batteries of peal bells tolled the heartbeat of every city and town.

A bell, despite its often immense size, is extremely fragile unless it is perfectly cast. Even a bell that has been cast using the most modern and scientific techniques may contain an imperfection; a small dent or an object touching against its surface while it is ringing may cause it to crack under the rapid vibration. English bellmakers experienced the greatest difficulty with bells cracking because of the greater force with which their bells are struck. A cracked bell cannot be repaired; only recasting will mend a damaged bell. While seeking to strengthen their bells, the John Taylor Company of Loughborough, England, accidentally discovered that it is the thickness of the rim or lip that determines the "strike tone" of a bell. The discovery was a tremendous breakthrough. With this knowledge bells could now be cast to produce a more or less predetermined tone. Today formulas for each note make more precise casting possible. Knowing that the thicker the rim, the sharper the note, bells are poured with the lip slightly thicker than the formula for that note would indicate. This creates a margin so that too sharp a tone can be "tuned" by shaving excess metal from the interior of the bell's rim. On the other hand, if the rim turned out to be too thin and the tone too flat, the bell would have to be melted down and recast.

Notwithstanding the many scientific advances that have been made, however, bellmaking remains very much a craftsman's art. The procedures for founding bells are closely guarded secrets held by individual craftsmen or small family-owned firms; some have been handed down by more than twenty generations of bellmakers. The Cathedral's fifty-three-bell carillon was cast by the John Taylor Company, now in its seventh century of

*Tuning a great bell at the foundry of the John Taylor Company in Loughborough, England.*

operation. Known as the finest bellmakers in the world, they nevertheless use no thermometers, no modern gauges. The old gentleman who stirs the molten metal with a wand of green willow somehow knows just when the temperature is right, and when the molten alloy is not too watery, not too thick. Then, after the bronze has been poured into the mold, it must be allowed to cool, or "freeze," at exactly the right rate. Speed up or slow down the process and the metal crystallizes imperfectly, the bell's tone suffering accordingly. Tuning, although no longer done by hand, is still done by ear. And tape recordings of fine old bells, when compared

129

to the sound of bells produced by the Taylor Company today, prove they are making them better all the time. But even the very best craftsmen find bellmaking an extremely difficult challenge, and no one, not even England's John Taylor himself, understands the entire process. The first attempt to cast the Cathedral's largest carillon bell failed because the mold broke just as the bronze was being poured. Twelve tons of liquid bronze had to be spilled out on the foundry floor; if it had hardened in the buckets, it would have ruined the equipment. After the metal had cooled, it was sawed up to be used again, and the process began anew. Ronald Barnes, the Cathedral's carillonneur for many years, summed up the bellmaker's art when he told me, "It's an amazingly steamy, sooty, beautiful madness."

The National Cathedral, the only church in the world that has both peal bells and a carillon in a single tower, came close to having no central bell tower at all. Europe is dotted with cathedrals that have elaborate west ends but no central tower. The problem is peculiar to Gothic cathedrals. Unlike most other buildings, they are completed bottom to top, section by section, and not, as is standard practice with most construction, built layer upon layer all at once. Thus when the construction, which always begins at the apse, reaches the crossing, it is necessary to decide whether to construct the nave and then return later to erect a central tower, or to build the central tower at the cost of delaying construction of the nave, possibly for years. The strongest argument for finishing the tower first is that once the nave is completed it is more difficult to build the central tower, as the nave and transepts present structural obstacles to the work. On the other hand, the reason for giving priority to the nave is that it provides a roof, and consequently makes it possible to use the cathedral—the reason for building the structure in the first place. In Old World cathedrals, the decision to put a cathedral to use more quickly won out; then, by the time the nave was completed it sometimes seemed unnecessary to go back and build the central tower—or sometimes, funds had run out, or times had changed. In the case of the National Cathedral, Dean Sayre persuaded the Building Committee to postpone finishing the nave and build the Gloria in Excelsis Tower first. He argued that the central tower would have tremendous dramatic power visually. Without the tower the majesty of the Cathedral's Mount St. Alban location, the highest in Washington, would be diminished; and the Cathedral's impact as a symbolic landmark would be greatly lessened. The Building Committee's decision was a brave one. Funds were short and expenditures on the tower might have meant postponing the nave for some time. But, together with Dean Sayre, they hoped that the visibility of the tower would encourage support for the nave. As it turned out, they were right. The nave is now completed and the central tower has become one of Washington's finest landmarks. It is also the home of the Cathedral bells.

That there would be a carillon had been determined long before the decision to go ahead with the central tower. In 1927 Bessie Juliet Kibbey, in making out her will, included the gift of a carillon for the Cathedral. Before leaving the funds, however, she did careful research on carillons, and specified exactly how many bells and exactly what weight. She even stipulated what inscriptions they would bear.

As for the peal bells, that is another matter. Dean Sayre, the story is told, had developed a fondness for change ringing when he was a student living in New York City's Upper West Side, where the playing of Riverside Church's Rockefeller Carillon, the world's largest, had distracted him from his studies. He had hoped that the Cathedral's bells would be a peal in the tradition of the great churches of England and the churches

*A bell for the Cathedral carillon leaves England.*

of the early American settlers. The Kibbey bequest for a carillon was a firm commitment. But Frohman said that there was no problem, there was enough room in the tower to accommodate both instruments–the carillon and a peal. The unusually large tower, he said, had space to spare! The dean urged the Building Committee to approve the two sets of bells. Funds were raised and sixty-three bells were commissioned to be cast.

In order to employ both of England's working foundries, the John Taylor Company, the foundry that almost a century ago revolutionized bellmaking, was chosen to cast the fifty-three bells for the carillon; the ten-bell ring went to the equally venerable firm of Mears and Stainbank of London, which had started in business during the reign of Queen Elizabeth I as the Whitechapel Bell Foundry, and had cast Big Ben and the original American Liberty Bell. The two bellmakers managed to coordinate their timing so well that all of the bells were ready to travel to the United States on the same ship. The peal bells and the call bell of the carillon, incidentally, are both tuned to D major so that, should the occasion ever arise, the two instruments would be compatible and could be rung in unison.

In the spring of 1963 all sixty-three bells arrived at the port of Baltimore. A crane, so large that telephone and electric wires had to be cleared from its path, was transported all the way from Philadelphia to Washington to hoist the bells to a platform built along the top of the north transept–the largest bell weighed twelve tons. The north side of the Cathedral's central tower had been left unbricked, and the bells were rolled in on logs, using the ancient Egyptian method. No one was certain that the transept roof could hold such an enormous load, so the dean ordered the Cathedral emptied, and the workers moving the bells, says carillonneur Barnes, "probably broke all records for speed."

## THE TEN-BELL RING

The highest chamber in the Gloria in Excelsis Tower, the highest point in Washington, houses the nation's most eloquent voice. There is no instrument of man that can move a city to joy or to sadness and mourning so effectively as the peal of the Cathedral's ten-bell ring. In England, unlike the Continent, one finds change bells everywhere, and it was the British who brought change ringing to North America, where it flourished during the colonial period. Paul Revere knew his way, even in total darkness, to the bell chamber in the steeple of Boston's Old North Church because he had for many years been captain of the church's change-ringing "band." It was unfortunate for change ringing that the Revolution, signaled by Revere's lanterns, caused so many of the young country's bells to be taken down and cast into cannon. And it is only within the past thirty-five or forty years that peal bells have once again been raised on this side of the Atlantic.

It was not until 1963 that the National Cathedral brought the first really large peal to the United States. Two years later the bells sounded the first full peal by an American band–no slight accomplishment when one realizes that change ringing is a craft entirely unto itself–there is simply nothing comparable.

Because of Frohman's generous allocation of space in the central tower, the Cathedral's set of change bells is one of only two in the world (the peal of England's Liverpool Cathedral is the other) with enough room to be hung in a full circle, or "in the round"–the classic arrangement for a peal. The bells are mounted on a steel frame in order of size. Each bell is connected to a wheel from which a rope falls through a hole in the floor to the ringers' chamber below. A pull on the rope sets the bell swinging, throwing the clapper against the rim.

The nature of a bell requires that it be

132

*The Ten-Bell Ring.*

swung evenly; an uneven swing makes it impossible to control the clapper, and the ring becomes chaotic. Thus for most ringing there is one band member assigned to each rope. That person is responsible for the sequence and rhythm of that particular bell, that particular note. The "pitch" and the volume of each peal bell is fixed and cannot change.

Starting with the bell in the "cocked" position, each ringer sets his bell in motion one after the other. Gradually all the ringers bring their bells into proper rhythm with the other bells. The ringer of the largest bell sets the pace because the heaviest bell is the slowest. Usually between 180 and 240 notes are rung per minute. Once all the bells are ringing at the same speed, the band falls into

an order of ringing called "rounds"; that is, every bell in sequence, each following the next larger one. For instance, bell #1 rings, bell #2 rings, and so on to bell #10, when the cycle begins all over again. In order to change the sequence of the ringing, one of the bells must speed up while another slows down, allowing them to trade places in the cycle. It is physically impossible, however, to speed up or slow down a bell quickly enough for it to advance or descend more than one position before its next ring. And so it is not possible to vary the sequence of notes (bells) quickly enough to play traditional harmonies. The music that has evolved instead is the "science" of change ringing. This is not conventional music but an orderly, mathematically predetermined variation in the se-

*High in the bell tower, members of the Cathedral change-ringing band during a practice session.*
(Photo by Morton Brotfman)

quence in which the bells are rung. A variation in the sequence is called a "change." The principal of change ringing is to play an entire "composition" without repeating any given sequence. For example, part of an arrangement known as "Plain Bob," here shown on four bells (although it is usually played on an even number of six or more bells), is rung in the following order:

| bell #, | bell #, | bell #, | bell # | |
|---------|---------|---------|--------|------------|
| 1 | 2 | 3 | 4 | (rounds) |
| 2 | 1 | 4 | 3 | 1st change |
| 2 | 4 | 1 | 3 | 2nd change |
| 4 | 2 | 3 | 1 | 3rd change |
| 4 | 3 | 2 | 1 | 4th change |
| 3 | 4 | 1 | 2 | 5th change |
| 3 | 1 | 4 | 2 | 6th change |
| 1 | 3 | 2 | 4 | 7th change |
| 1 | 3 | 4 | 2 | 8th change |

With four bells there would be twenty-four changes before "Plain Bob" returns to "rounds," ending the arrangement.

With six bells there are 720 possible changes. With the Cathedral's bells there are more than 3.5 million possible changes! A "full peal" consists of 5,000 or more consecutive changes and requires over three hours to perform. To date more than sixteen full peals have been rung at the National Cathedral. A peal is by far the most dramatic event in the life of a bell tower–at the Cathedral the tons of swinging bronze, heard from Bethesda to the White House, literally set the great tower swaying!

When the decision was made to install the ten-bell ring, no one involved fully realized just how complicated the art of change ringing was. It is impractical for changes to be scored, as is other music. It would be impossible to follow. Thus, even if he has had musical training, a change ringer must learn the craft from scratch; it normally takes several years to become a proficient ringer. The Cathedral's bellmaster, Rick Dirksen, told me that even with daily practice, it takes at least two years to become a capable band member. Just handling the pull rope is tricky and requires special experience. More than a few bell ringers have had bones broken when their concentration lapsed and they were caught in the rope and hurled ceilingward by the force of the swinging bell. In addition, every member of a band is dependent upon every other member. If one person loses the rhythm, he throws the next person off, and then the next person, and so on. To help the ringers keep the pace, a bell "captain" calls out the changes and monitors the speed of the bells. "There are times," bellmaster Dirksen told me, "when one of the ringers gets out of step and the captain must improvise changes to prevent a 'false' ring (the repeat of a change). If a ringer gets lost and you don't catch him in time, it's bedlam."

## THE CARILLON

Though I had often heard and admired the bells played at New York's Riverside Church, I had never had a chance to see a carillon—tens of tons of bells all rung from a pianolike keyboard by a single musician, without assistance from any form of energy other than his own. Carl Tucker, the Cathedral's crackerjack-of-all-trades, who is also an incurable romantic with a sense of drama, took me up to see the carillon the first time we met. I was absolutely astounded. Fifty-three bells clamped tightly to an enormous steel frame fill the two-story room. Tucker motioned for me to duck inside the largest bell. This bell, called the bourdon, is big enough to shelter a table and chairs for four. Every portion of the bronze inner surface is rifled by turns of the tuner's lathe. Assuring me it wouldn't be too loud, Tucker gently pushed the huge clapper against the bell's lip; instantly I was in the very middle of an E flat. With my hand I could feel the powerful vibrations long after I could hear them.

In the midst of the carillon, surrounded by 130,000 pounds of steel frame and bronze bells, sits the carillonneur's cabin. This small heated and sound-dampened room houses the keyboard, the heart of the carillon. Each key is connected by weighted wire to the clapper of a bell. The clappers of the heavier bells are also connected to pedals so they can be played by foot as well as by hand. The keys are in chromatic order with half tones slightly raised, as on a piano. The mechanism is so efficient and direct that the clapper travels exactly the same distance as the key. The harder the key is struck, the louder the volume of the bell. Cathedral carillonneur Ronald Barnes explained to me that the mechanical action of the keys makes it possible to vary each note because of the immediacy of control it gives the player. "I have heard," says Barnes, "two musicians sit down, one after the other, and play the same piece with the same rhythm—one sounds beautiful, while the other makes the bells seem out of tune. On a well-built instrument, like the Cathedral's, if it is in excellent condition, the carillonneur's touch is everything."

Because the number of bells, and thus the number of tones, varies from carillon to carillon, there is no such thing as a standard carillon keyboard. The Cathedral's carillon, with a range of four and a half octaves, is twice the size of most instruments of its kind. As a result very little carillon music is published, and still fewer original carillon compositions are written. "When you have to play over fifty recitals a year," says Barnes, "the only way to have a large enough repertory is to arrange and compose your own music, suited to your particular carillon." And to a large extent the individual carillon dictates the music that can be played upon it. The keyboard permits complex, rapid harmonies—so long as they do not require the carillonneur to play quickly on the heavy brass notes. "If you choose a piece that contains too much bass so that some of it must be omitted," Barnes told me, "determining how much can be cut away without destroying the composition is a matter of taste and judgment." Another problem is that there is no way to dampen the bells. Once struck, a note sounds until it slowly dies away. For this reason, Barnes feels the carillon is particularly suited to music with strong rhythmic definition, such as Elizabethan dances. "Passages that are too fast tend to smear the sounds together." Barnes also mentions, however, that a skillful musician can use the sonority of the bells to advantage, creating effects such as those found in the misty veiled music of Claude Debussy.

Carillonneurs speak of the National Cathedral's carillon as one of the most versatile and sensitive instruments in the world today. The bells are exceptionally fine, cast when the Taylor Company was in its prime. The placing of the bells and the mechanical design of the carillon is enormously successful. And the carillon is still in absolutely perfect working condition, though it was installed almost twenty years ago. Much of the credit goes to Richard Strauss, the carillonneur who has taken over for Ronald Barnes. Strauss is also one of the finest carillon craftsmen in North America, a specialist in restoration as well as in the maintenance of the huge instruments. "Because of Strauss," Barnes, says, "the Cathedral's carillon has an even finer 'touch' today than when it was installed."

The fact that the Cathedral has paid such exceptional attention to keeping its carillon in outstanding working order makes the instrument increasingly valuable to the world of music. At one time there were hundreds of carillons in Europe, but the ravages of time and lack of money are slowly destroying many of the carillons throughout the world. Unfortunately, also, most were in the Low Countries, where the wonderfully flat terrain became Europe's favorite battlefield. As war followed war, more and more bells were taken down and melted to make weapons; every time peace returned, some—but not all—would be replaced. At the start of World War II there were still over one hundred carillons left.

When the Nazis invaded Belgium and the Netherlands, they ordered the very best bells marked with a K (for *Kunst*, meaning "work of art") and promised those would be preserved; all of the rest would be smelted for war. The Dutch and the Belgian promptly painted K's on *all* of the bells. The Nazis retaliated by taking virtually all of them down and shipping them by rail to Germany. But at every whistle-stop and every time one of the trains slowed for a steep grade, patriotic Lowlanders pushed bells off the flatcars and hid them by burying them alongside the track. Many trains arrived in Germany completely empty of bells. After the war the hidden bells were dug up and put back in towers, but even so, many bells were lost. (An interesting aside is that the Germans discovered many of the bells were cast so well that they couldn't be broken, in the usual way, with a sledgehammer—in fact, the Germans had great difficulty breaking them at all, and finally had to build a special machine to do the job!)

In the United States virtually all of the carillons, both those installed more than forty years ago and many of the newer ones, have deteriorated—some to the point where the bells are liable to fall. Though the bronze bells themselves will last for a millenium, the mechanical parts and the steel frame can seriously corrode in less than half a century. For instance, the best clappers are made of malleable iron, and even though they are originally painted for protection, the paint is gradually worn off at the strike point. When this happens they begin to rust. If the carillon is not played often enough, the rust builds up, and even a little rust can destroy the tone of the ring.

Every part of the Cathedral's carillon functions as smoothly today as when it was first installed in 1964; every key is like new. And with regular weekly recitals (Barnes told me they may soon have as many as three a week), plus services and special occasions, it is not likely that rust will form on the clappers of the National Cathedral for some time.

# APPENDIXES

# INITIAL REPORT TO THE BUILDING COMMITTEE
## OF THE NATIONAL CATHEDRAL
### BY ARCHITECTS BODLEY AND VAUGHAN
### ACCOMPANYING THEIR PRELIMINARY DRAWINGS
### 1907

In laying the drawings of our design for the new Cathedral before you we would offer a few explanatory remarks, calling attention to the general character of the building, and to some of its distinctive features.

In style it is, as was wisely desired, "Gothic" of the fourteenth century–a style of architecture, as we think, the most beautiful that the world has ever seen. In its dimensions it will be larger than most of the Cathedrals in England, or on the Continent. The total length is 476 feet, and the total width 132 feet. These are the external dimensions. The height to the ridge line of the roof is 130 feet; while to the internal apex of the vaulting it is 93 feet.

The Central Tower will rise 220 feet from the ground. The plan is that of Nave and Aisles, Transepts, Choir and two Chapels. Double Aisles are planned for the Nave. These latter will be especially useful for Monuments and Memorial windows and Tablets. The Choir terminates in an apsidal Sanctuary. The building will be vaulted in stone throughout.

The lighting of the interior is designed to have a fine effect, being lit by ample Clerestory windows. The light, thus coming from so high a level, will, in your bright climate, be striking and uplifting. There are lower windows in the Aisles; but they are quite subordinate. Then there will be a striking effect of light in the "Sanctuary," or eastern part of the Choir. For there is to be a large window both on the north and south sides, coming lower down, but much out of sight, being in the depth of thick walls. These windows will be 65 feet long. Light will be given by them to the Apse, in an especial and striking manner. It is for this important effect of light that we propose to have no Chapel at the far eastern end, in the more usual position when a Choir-aisle runs round the east end.

This plan has the advantage, too, of giving an interior of which the whole length is seen on entering at the west end; thus, adding to the perspective, and to the impressive effect of the building.

We propose two Chapels at the ends of the Choir-aisles, the south one could be the Lady Chapel and the other the Chapel of SS. Peter and Paul, who give title to the Cathedral; or the north Chapel could be the Chapel of St. John the Evangelist, the two Chapels thus symbolizing the scene of Calvary. An aisle terminating in a mere wall always has a poor and an unsatisfactory effect. It will be a great advantage to have Chapels here at the eastern ends of the two aisles, each with their Screens and Altar and their Reredos. The eye will be attracted down the "long-drawn aisles" to these Chapels. We think there should be no windows at the end of these two aisles, for light there would take the eye and have a disturbing effect. The Apse with the effect of light there that we have spoken of, should be the leading and the impressive feature. The two long windows will not be seen until one gets opposite to them, while their effect of light-giving, as we have said, will be exceedingly good. The exterior of the Apse, unhidden by a further building, will be commanding in its lofty proportion, and will make a very conspicuous landmark eastward, crowning the hill with its cluster of many pinnacles.

The Chapels at the ends of the aisles would be used for people during Choir services, and will thus afford accommodation. An isolated Lady Chapel would be a place *per se* and not useful for those attending the services conducted in the Choir, nor would it add to the internal effect. It is for these reasons that we have planned the Chapels where shown, and no separated Lady-Chapel. The Chapel in the position shown will be bright with its south windows. There will be a gleam of light from it.

Another feature to which we would call attention is, that it is proposed to have a broad soffit, 9 feet 6 inches wide, forming the eastern arch of the central Tower. This deep sweep of soffit, or under side of the arch, we propose to have carved with figures of Angels, arranged in a suitable design. It would be, as it were, an Angelic canopy over the Rood and will be an effective treatment. It would recall the words, "which things the Angels desire to look into," and the words of an old hymn, "Inter Angelos laudamus Te," "We praise Thee amidst the Angels." The Angels could each hold a scroll with the words, "Sursum corda," the key-note, as it were, of the whole building.

Beyond this arch would be the Choir and the Sanctuary. In the latter, could be represented our Lord, in glory, blessing, in the upper part of a lofty and dignified Reredos.

The stained-glass Clerestory windows, as they could be placed, should consist of single Figures, for they are too high up to contain "subjects." The glass should have finely-coloured figures on a light, silvery ground. These windows could set forth the history of religion in the world, beginning, in the Nave, with some of the Old Testament worthies, Prophets and Kings; and so on to Malachi, the last of the Prophets, and St. John Baptist, and then to the Apostles and Saints of the New Testament, and to many of later Christian years. We think, however, that all represented should be worthies of the Old Testament or Christian Saints, recognized as such. The great Church, however, will not have any very especial need of coloured glass. It would be desirable, however, to have it in the south windows of the Lady Chapel, or the sunlight may be too strong there. It would be well, too, to have it at the east end windows of the Apse. But there are other things for which gifts would be more desirable, before the glass, in point of time. There are many stone statues desirable, and many carved subjects.

We have alluded to the outer aisles as being available for monuments. Here there could be placed mural tablets as memorials, and Brasses round the walls; and indeed, "altar-tombs" with effigies, one in each space, could be placed as opportunity occurs. The Bishop reminds us that as Washington Cathedral is at the Capital of the Nation, and will inspire combined religious and patriotic feelings, it would be well, in some parts of the Cathedral, if place could be made for statues, bas-reliefs and other works, commemorating great American heroes and statesmen of the United States, and historical incidents of Colonial times and after the Revolution, which are dear to the hearts of American people. This could be easily arranged and suitable places found.

The site is a remarkably fine one, very commanding and beautiful. The Cathedral will be a conspicuous object from the Capitol and other parts of the city. When complete, with its surrounding buildings, it will be "as a city set on a hill."

Approaching the west end by a triple avenue of trees, those visiting the Cathedral will find three lofty open arches, the central one wider and much higher, than the other two. These lead to three wide vaulted spaces to be used as large porches or porticoes, and so on to the three recessed west doorways. The central portico could be treated richly internally with arcading and many statues and carved subjects. These statues would be such as the Major and Minor Prophets, etc., etc., David and other worthies, all old Testament characters, ending with St. John Baptist, who could be turning to the central entrance, where, in its midst, there could be the figure of our Lord blessing those who enter. Below could be inscribed "Lux Mundi," or "Salvator Mundi." St. John Baptist could hold a scroll inscribed with his "Ecce Agnus Dei." The two subordinate side entrances at the west end could have statues of St. Peter and St. Paul, one in each, and, possibly, some scenes from their lives, at the sides of these porches internally.

While the exterior surroundings of this lower part of the west end are massive (the richer part being kept for the top of the Towers "whose glory is in their height"), the interior of this central portico can be rich and stately, and be made beautiful with its many figures and pictorially carved subjects. It may be a very "Testament in stone," beginning with Adam and Eve in the Garden of Paradise, and ending with St. John the Baptist preaching in the Wilderness. Other statues, outside this great porch, and in different parts of the Cathedral, could be many and various Christian Saints and heroes and worthies, and possibly some few especial modern ones, e.g., and more especially, Washington and Penn. Suitable statues may be added to the building as time goes on. Brackets could be provided for them from the first. In passing, may we say that all and every gift should not be in kind, but that the money should be given for each gift, and that all things given should be approved by the Architects. Incongruous things may be given, with the best intentions, that may be out of character and without harmony with the surroundings. This is most important. It is astonishing what harm a single note out of harmony will do; and so with every detail of furniture, or colour; everything must be in keeping and manifest the same intention, drawn from the same inspiration.

Passing along the north side of the Cathedral externally, we would speak of the height of the walls, the interest of the window tracery in the Clerestory, the massive, but not too heavy, flying buttresses and pinnacles; of the light and shade given by them, and the bands of rich work in the outer aisles, windows and niches and the carved Canticles of the Church's Matins and Evensong, and the traceried parapets. Then, passing these, we get to the North Transept, with its protected entrance up many steps, and its high turrets and Rose window. Then to the vestries for Bishop, Clergy and choir, and so to the lofty east end, with its apsidal termination and its bold flying buttresses and pinnacles. "Sanctus" will be carved on each of the three sides of the Apse parapet.

Coming round to the south side we see the outside of the Lady-Chapel, and a somewhat similar to the northern, but varied, South Transept, with its different Rose window, Doorway, with figures set round it, and its many steps necessitated by the fall of the ground. Then to the Baptistery, a lofty stone octagonal erection, with its seven windows and high roof, surmounted by a metal Cross. The effect of this Baptistery, externally, will be good. It will be varied in its light and shade, being octagonal, and it will stand out from the great mass of the great Church, with its gilded Cross at the Apex, catching the light, and its many flying buttresses and its connecting passage.

Such will be the leading features of the exterior, all of commanding proportions.

And now to enter the Cathedral at the west, through the great portico we have spoken of, and through the shelter of an internal oak lobby.

The first impression will be the continuous height of the main, or central part, namely, the Nave, Choir and Apse. The next, and nearly as powerful a one, will be the width; for with the outer aisles and the double range of columns on either side, and the Transepts, the effect of the width will be very considerable. Then, as we hope and think may be confidently anticipated, will be the uplifting proportion of the whole–the tall piers and arches, with the Triforium and the lofty Clerestory, and the rich and full, tree-like, branching vaulting, springing from soaring verticle shafts, rising from the floor, and of slender diameter. For pains have been taken to make the interior effect a striking and an aspiring one. Then the eye will be taken up to the Rood and to the broad enriched soffit of the easternmost arch of the Tower, with its carved Angels, and to the Rood, which it frames; to the Screen, with its delicate open work, only veiling the beyond, with a very transparent veil, to the dark oak, or other wood, of the Choir Stalls with their fretted canopies; and so to the bright Sanctuary with, perhaps rays of light from a southern-like sun, lighting, but half veiling with light, the Reredos, with its sculptured Saints and the Christ in glory, blessing, above all.

The Triforium will be continued round the Apse, knitting all together into, as we hope and believe it will be, an elevating, harmonious whole *ad majorem gloriam Dei.* Such has been the opportunity to be afforded us at Washington. It is, after all, the interior that will be of the greatest inspiring interest and of the chief importance for, the edification of the worshippers.

With regard to the position for the pulpit we would say that the transepts, as deep as is desirable, will hold a good many people, so that to place the pulpit at one of the great piers of the Tower may be best. But another pulpit could very well be put in the centre of the length of the Nave, for especial occasions, as well as one for the Choir, which will be needed, east of the stalls, and not far from opposite the Bishop's "throne" or Choir seat.

The Bishop's sanctuary seat and faldstool would be in the window recess, on the north side of the Sanctuary, the most western of the long windows spoken of.

The Baptistery, as we have said, will

afford a pleasing interior with its lofty, slender central column and vaulted roof. Externally it will look well, giving the planes of the octagonal plan to take varied light and shade and standing out against the great Minster.

We have arranged two ample staircases to the Triforium; for an especial occasion that will hold a number of people attending the services.

One word as to the treatment of the Building as regards its richness, or the reverse. We think the drawings show that it is amply rich enough. That there should be plenty of surface of massive stone ashlar is most desirable for all good architecture, especially with a building so large as this. A small building may be rich all over, but it is beneath the dignity of a great one. For a large building, if well designed, has an instinctive dignity and a grandeur about it that may well dispense with too lavish exuberance of ornament. Again, there should be concentration of richness and not a spreading of it all over a building. We think our building is rich enough. Internally, the Screen and the Reredoses, the Stalls and the Bishop's throne, could be as rich as any donor likes to make them; but we think the fabric is sufficiently ornate, taking it as a whole. That it will be impressive by its size and dignity we doubt not. As we have said, we have suggested a good many statues which will give much interest to the building. They could be added by degrees.

On the central Tower we propose to have a band of large Angels, each holding a scroll with a word of the "Gloria in excelsis Deo," etc. They will give a rich effect and teach a constant song of praise. This band of Angels will be an original treatment, not before attempted, certainly not on this scale. The figures would be about 10 ft. high.

The Organ, we think, should be placed where shown. It is to be hoped that an Organ on one side may be found to be sufficient. It would be best if only on the one side. There could, however, be two if thought necessary. An Organ on the Screen, even if divided, would interfere with the effect of the Rood and the view eastward. We do not recommend it there.

Many details for the stone work are already prepared and progress could very soon be made.

There remains the question of the stone to be used, and it is a very important one, for stone ashlar would be used both inside and outside the building. Knowing, as we do, the good effect of churches built entirely of a good light red stone, and the cold look that white stone has, we cannot but recommend the use of a good red one. It should be by no means brown, but of a good, soft-looking, rosy tint. We would mention Hoar Cross Church, near Burton-on-Trent, as a church where red stone is used with good effect, and the interior of Clumber Church, near Worksop. Lord Burton is now building a church at Burton all of red stone.

The red stone we should use would not be too dark, or at all heavy-looking. With red stone a church has a warmth of colour, and a look of the absence of newness, that is very satisfactory. Details for red stone are best bolder, and therefore less expensive, than those suitable for a white stone. Specimens of stones are laid before you. Our advice is that the best of the red stone be used. We believe it would be entirely approved of if decided upon.

It does not seem necessary to have many steps at the west end. The ground does not require them. We think about four would be enough. To have many steps there would be to raise the fabric needlessly. There must, however, be a flight of many steps at both the Transept entrances, as shown on plans.

The pavement of the interior should be of American marbles–simpler in the Nave and Aisles, richer in the Choir, and especially rich in the Sanctuary.

The work is a great one. Its importance, from every point of view, is great. It is a grand opportunity. We shall be glad to do what we can to expedite the work, and hope it may be taken in hand soon.

Lastly, our desire and our hope is to raise your great Cathedral that it may inspire hearts with a joyful devotion, and unite them in the carrying out of a great monumental, National and religious work in your Capital of Washington.

Faithfully yours,

G. F. Bodley, R.A., F.S.A.
7, Gray's Inn Square
London

H. Vaughan,
Boston,
America

*Note:* We have not designed a Chapter-House, understanding that it is contemplated to build a large Hall for Church meetings and gatherings, etc. Such a Hall could serve as a Chapter-House, or there could be one attached to it of the dimensions required for Chapter purposes. The desirable offices could be built in connection with this large Hall.

This Building should follow on the completion of the Cathedral, which is of first import. The Hall and other building should be designed to be in harmony with the Cathedral, though they should have a more Domestic character of Gothic architecture. They should not be too high, so as not to interfere with the views of the Cathedral itself. But it will be an artistic advantage to have well-designed buildings near it. We should be glad to design such erections. There would be ample and good space on the site for them. We think they would be best on the ground to the southwest of the Cathedral, approached from the avenue, and not far from it. There could be rooms for a caretaker and other offices.

But such a building should not hamper or delay the building of the great Church. It would be very advisable to put in the whole of the foundations of the Cathedral–advisable for the practical purpose of construction. That should be the first part of the work. To raise the whole super-structure together, gradually, would be much the best for the building construction, if it should be possible to do so. The bonding of the main building together would be a great and real practical advantage. Temporary vestries could be built. The Baptistery, the carving and all the furniture could be postponed; but the more of the main fabric that may be built continuously the better it will be for the work. A vaulted building of this scale requires ample abutments. We cannot but strongly advise the building of the whole together if it is found to be possible.

## A LIST OF KNOWN CATHEDRAL SCULPTORS AND CARVERS
(In addition to sculptors of stone, I have included Cathedral sculptors in other mediums.)

| | | | |
|---|---|---|---|
| Louis Amateis | James Earle Fraser | Tony Luciani | Peter Rockwell |
| Percy Bryant Baker | Mary Aldrich Fraser | William M. McVey | William F. Ross |
| Theodore C. Barbarosa | Stinius Fredriksen | Donald Miller | Constantine Seferlis |
| Marian Brackenridge | Daniel Chester French | Enrique Monjo | Joseph Servos |
| Gino Bresciani | Carl Frey | Roger Morigi | William Conrad Severson |
| Carl L. Bush | G. M. Galloway | Carl C. Mose | William B. Shackleford |
| Ettore Cadorin | John Guarente | Thomas Nicholls | Andrea Sichi |
| Granville Carter | Salvatore Gussio | George M. O'Toole | Stephen Sykes |
| Hazel Clere | Walker K. Hancock | Paul Palumbo | Anthony Toffoli |
| Joseph A. Coletti | Malcolm Harlow | Vincent Palumbo | George Tsutakawa |
| Couch and Haid Company | Frederick (Rick) E. Hart | Andrew Pennucci | Don Turano |
| Oswald Del Frate | Herbert Haseltine | Luca Petrini | Frank Vereka |
| Bernard Del Negro | Nathaniel Hitch | Lawrence Pfefferly | Carl Vogel |
| John J. Early | Herbert Houck | Patrick J. Plunkett | Heinz Warneke |
| John Evans | Paul Maximilien Landowski | Edward Ratti | Charles Wood |
| Italo Fanfani | Lee Lawrie | Joseph Ratti | Frank Zic |
| John (Jack) Guido Fanfani | Angelo Lualdi | Sani Rizzo | Frank Zucchetti |

## ARTISTS IN GLASS AND THEIR WORKS

| Name of Artist and Window | Window in Memorial | Location in the National Cathedral |
|---|---|---|
| *Brenda Belfield* | | |
| Commissioned to design forty-four lancet windows | | West facade |
| Commissioned to design two windows | To Hide Suzki | Northwest turret stair |
| | To Anna Eisenmenger | Northwest turret stair |
| *Albert Birkle* | | |
| The Church at Rome | To Virginia Martin | East side of the south transept |
| The Twenty-third Psalm | To Euginia Bell and Hanson Lee Dulin | North outer aisle of the nave |
| Architects and Sculptors | To George Allen | Above Glover Bay in the nave |
| Coming Great Church | To Frances Berg Kemmer | South transept clerestory |
| *Ervin Bossanyi* | | |
| War and Peace | To Woodrow Wilson | Wilson Bay in the nave |
| The Women's Window | To the devoted Women of the National Cathedral Association | National Cathedral Bay in the nave |
| *Wilbur Burnham* | | |
| Theology of Baptism | | South wall of the baptistry |
| History of Baptism | To Rahel O'Fon and Edward Davies | Southwest wall of the baptistry |
| Lee and Jackson | | South side of the nave |
| Joan of Arc | To Ethelyn Garratt Talbott | Above Kellogg Bay in the nave |
| Education | To Benjamin Riegel | East wall of the north transept |

| Name of Artist and Window | Window in Memorial | Location in the National Cathedral |
|---|---|---|
| The Prayer Book | To Samuel and Corra Hull Rummage | West clerestory of the north transept |
| Law | To William Edgar Edmonston | East clerestory of the north |
| Physicians | To Dr. Elmer Burkitt Freeman | East clerestory, north transept |
| Angel of Annunciation | | South choir clerestory |
| Jacob Wrestling with the Angel | To George H. and Jane James Cook | North choir clerestory |
| The Garden of Eden | To George H. and Jane James Cook | North choir clerestory |
| Music and the 100th Psalm | To Margaret Suter | Crypt stairway outside bride's room |
| "A Decorative Window" | To Margaret Suter | Crypt stairway outside bride's room |
| Jacob's Ladder | To Jessie Sayre Wilson | North transept balcony stair |
| Worcester, Massachusetts | To the town of Worcester from its Citizens | South transept balcony |
| *Wilbur Burnham and Joseph Reynolds* | | |
| Crucifixion | To Josephine Wheelwright Rust | Apse |
| Christ in Majesty | To Harry Lee Rust | Apse |
| Resurrection | To Gwynn Wheelwright Rust | Apse |
| A Church Triumphant | To Mary M. Kingsland | South rose window |
| Bartholomew and Philip | To Mabel Stanwood Emery | South transept lancet |
| Andrew and James | To Lillian M. Oakley | South transept lancet |
| Luke and Thomas | | South transept lancet |
| The Authors of the Constitution | To George Shepley Selfridge | Above the slype entrance |
| The Declaration of Independence | | Above the slype door |
| *Nicola D'Ascenzo* | | |
| The Woman of Samaria | To Henry Heyer | Holy Spirit Chapel |
| *Fredrica Fields* | | |
| "The Little Window" | | South transept west turret |
| *Evie Hone* | | |
| The Raising of Jairus' Daughter | To Margot de Zuberbuhler | The Baptistry |
| *Hans Kaiser* | | |
| The Dickenson Memorial | | West facade |
| Frohman Bay Windows (In Commission) | | North wall of the nave |

| Name of Artist and Window | Window in Memorial | Location in the National Cathedral |
|---|---|---|
| *Thomas Kempe and Company* (London) | | |
| Benedictus | | Above the south crypt entrance |
| Magnificat | | Above the north crypt choir |
| Samuel and David | | North crypt aisle |
| Daniel and Malachai | | North crypt aisle |
| John the Baptist | | East wall of the north crypt aisle |
| Joshua and Moses | | South crypt aisle |
| Isaac and Abraham | | East end of the south crypt aisle |
| John the Evangelist | | East wall of the south crypt aisle |
| *Thomas Kempe and Company –Walter Tower* | | |
| Incarnation of the Son of God | To Bishop Satterlee | Five windows in Bethlehem Chapel |
| *Charles Lawrence–* Commissioned to design the Healing Arts Window | | |
| *Rowan LeCompte and Irene LeCompte* | | |
| The Humanitarian Window | To Mabel Thorp Boardman and her Family | Boardman Bay |
| America the Beautiful | To Edwin Bettelheim, Jr. | North wall of the nave |
| Angel of the Nativity | To James Sheldon | Choir clerestory |
| Man's Search for God | To Charles C. Glover, Sr. and Annie Cunningham Glover | Apse clerestory |
| Transfiguration | To Arthur Ambler, Jr. | Apse clerestory |
| Wesley | To The Parents of Chaplain Robert Stretch and his sister Florence | Southwest turret |
| St. Phocas of Sinope | To the Reverend Nathaniel Manning | Southwest turret |
| Manning Window | To the Reverend Nathaniel Manning | West turret of the south transept |
| St. Dunstan | To the Reverend Nathaniel Manning | St. Dunstan's Chapel |
| St. Dunstan's Seal | To the Reverend Nathaniel Manning | St. Dunstan's Chapel stair |
| The Angel of Deliverance | To Richard Furneaux and Kate Darby Watson | Choir clerestory |
| *Rowan LeCompte* | | |
| The Childhood of Jesus | | Apse clerestory |

| Name of Artist and Window | Window in Memorial | Location in the National Cathedral |
|---|---|---|
| The Maryland Window | To Anna Campbell Ellicott, Charlotte Campbell Nelson and Ella Campbell Smythe | Ellicott Bay |
| The Woman in the Sun<br>Poets and Writers | To Barclay Adams Howard and Beale Richardson Howard | Above the Folger Bay |
| The Creation | To William Douglas Sloane and Malcolm Douglas Sloane | West rose window |
| The Philosophers | To Charles Norton | North nave aisle |

(Presently LeCompte is at work on a commission to complete windows for the South nave clerestory and the choir clerestory.)

*Robert Lewis*

| | | |
|---|---|---|
| The History of the Presbyterian Church | To Andrew Mellon | South wall of the nave |

*Robert Pinart*–Lincoln

| | | |
|---|---|---|
| Bay Window in Commission | | North wall of the nave |

*John Piper*

| | | |
|---|---|---|
| The Churchill Window | To Winston Churchill | West facade |

*Edward Renggli*

| | | |
|---|---|---|
| Christianity | To G. Lewis Jones | South transept |

*Joseph Reynolds*

| | | |
|---|---|---|
| Agriculture and Maritime | To William Green | Above the World Peace Bay |
| Artisans and Craftsmen | To Samuel Gompers | Above the Wilson Memorial |
| The Canada Window | To Dean George Carl Fitch Bratenahl | North transept |
| South America | To Bishop James Edward Freeman | North transept clerestory |
| Religious Painters | To Francis Eudorah Pope | Above the Mellon Bay |
| The Church in Jerusalem | To Henry St. George Tucker | South transept clerestory |
| Good and Faithful Servant | To William Mott Steuart | East turret of the south transept |
| Immortality | | East turret of the south transept |

*Reynolds, Francis and Rohnstock (and Setti)*

| | | |
|---|---|---|
| The Freedom Windows | The central window is a memorial to John Upshur Morehead | War Memorial Chapel |
| Universal Peace | To Frank Billings Kellogg | North wall of the nave |
| Florence Nightingale | | Above the parclose stair |
| Daniel | To Harvey Rowland, the younger | North transept |
| The Angel at the Tomb | To Edward G. Drake | Resurrection Chapel |

150

| Name of Artist and Window | Window in Memorial | Location in the National Cathedral |
|---|---|---|
| Beloved Disciple | To Raymond McDonald Yarbrough | Resurrection Chapel |
| Mary Rushing from the Tomb | To Maude Beall Ford | Resurrection Chapel |
| *Patrick Reyntiens* | | |
| The Armed Forces | To Thomas Dresser White | North wall of the nave |
| Servants of God | To William Pratt | North aisle of the nave |
| *Lawrence Saint* | | |
| The Last Judgment | To Mrs. Rose J. Coleman | North rose window |
| Foretellers of Judgment | To James Parmalee<br>To Myron T. Herrick<br>To Matthew Fontaine Maury | North rose lancets |
| Moses | To Sarah Clark Kauffman | North transept, west wall |
| Deborah and Barak | To Amaryllis Gillett | North transept, west wall |
| Truth | To William Thomas Hildrup, Jr. | Parclose stair |
| Falsehood | To William Thomas Hildrup, Jr. | Parclose stair |
| Miracles | To Lucien Jones | St. John's Chapel |
| Miracles | To William Marvin Jones | St. John's Chapel |
| Miracles | To Norman Prince | St. John's Chapel |
| The Parable Windows | | St. Mary's Chapel |
| *Earl Edward Sanborn and Lawrence Saint* | | |
| Angels of Deliverance (reworked in 1971 by Rowan LeCompte) | To Mary Lawton | Choir clerestory |
| Angels of Revelation | To Annie A. Cole | Choir clerestory |
| Angels of Resurrection | To Mrs. Alvin T. Hert and sisters | Choir clerestory |
| *Earl Edward Sanborn* | | |
| Te Deum | To Mrs. Percy R. Pyne | Apse |
| *Napoleon Setti* | | |
| Industrial and Social Reform | To Philip Murray | North nave aisle |
| Musicians and Composers | To Henry A. Hurlburt, Jr. | South nave aisle |
| Spirit of Law | To Charles Warren | South nave aisle |
| Nourse Window | To James Nourse | East turret of the south transept |
| *Henry Lee Willet* | | |
| Samuel and David | To Roland Leslie Taylor, Jr. | Children's Chapel |
| International Peace and Unity | To Henry and Margaret Stuyvesant Rutherford White | North nave aisle |

| Name of Artist and Window | Window in Memorial | Location in the National Cathedral |
|---|---|---|
| Good Shepherd | To Thomas Oliver and Fanny Randle Stokes | Parclose stair |
| Western Exploration | John Clifford Folger and Katherine Dulin Folger and children | South nave aisle |
| *Rodney Winfield* | | |
| Scientists and Technicians (The Space Window) | "In honor of the first trip to the moon" | South nave aisle |

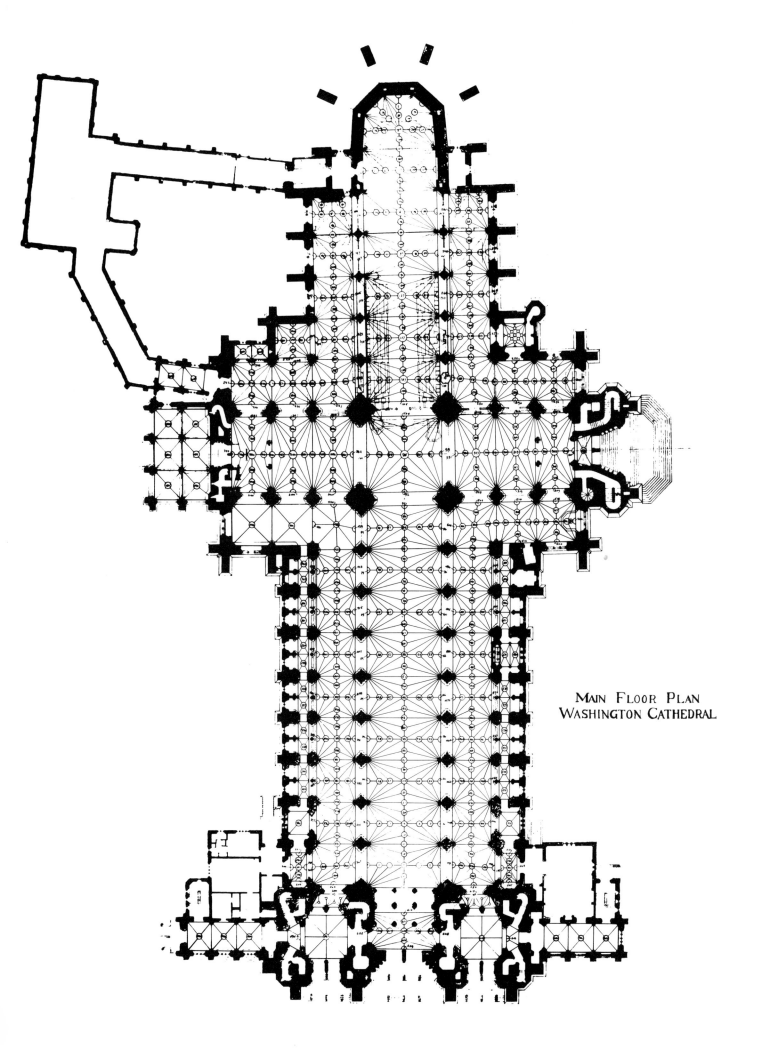

MAIN FLOOR PLAN
WASHINGTON CATHEDRAL

# A GOTHIC GLOSSARY

AMBULATORY–The aisle surrounding or on the side of a chapel or chamber, such as the apse, nave, or choir.

APSE–The vaulted, semicircular superstructure that forms the end of the sanctuary, usually the easternmost section of a cathedral.

ARCADE–A symmetrical range of columns and arches, with all of the ribs of the same curvature.

ASHLAR–A cut stone block used for building horizontal walls.

BAND–A group of ten or more musicians trained to ring changes on peal bells.

BARREL VAULT–A tunnel-like series of arches.

BAS-RELIEF–Sculpture in low relief, usually no more than half images.

BAY–An area enclosed by two pillars and a section of wall sometimes with an arch–often, as in the nave, furnished as a prayer room for one or two people.

BOSS–The carvings on the base of the stones at the intersections of the ribs.

BUTTRESS–An exterior-projecting masonry structure that supports the weight of wall and roof and bears the thrust of archwork.

CAPITAL–The head, crown, or top section of a column or pier. Gothic capitals are frequently carved.

CATHEDRAL–A church containing the official seat or chair of a bishop; this chair is called a cathedra.

CENTERING–The temporary wooden scaffolding that supports arch stonework until the mortar sets and the completed arch can stand on its own.

CLERESTORY–The highest windowed level on the outside walls of the main section of a cathedral, providing most of the daylight illumination for the nave and the sanctuary.

CLOSE–The grounds that surround a cathedral.

COLUMBARIA–The vaults beneath the nave where cinerary urns are stored in specially constructed recesses.

CORBEL–A triangular-shaped stone projecting from a wall to provide support for a molding, a beam, or the like. Corbels are often decoratively carved.

COURSE–A horizontal range of stone, a layer in the construction of a masonry wall.

CROCKET–Stone carved, usually in the shape of a curled leaf or other foliage, as an ornament on the multipolygonal edge of a pinnacle or spire.

CROSSING–The area framed by the intersection of the nave, the transepts, and the choir.

CRYPT–The subterranean level beneath the main body of a cathedral.

FABRICATOR–The craftsman who constructs the windows of stained glass, which the artist designs.

FINIAL–The decorative uppermost section of a pinnacle, usually decorated with crockets.

FLYING BUTTRESS–An exterior arch that transfers the thrust of structural archwork and roof to the buttress.

GANG–A stone-setting crew composed of a mason and two helpers.

GARGOYLE–A fantastic figure carved in a stone, through the mouth of which passes a spout that directs rainwater out away from the walls.

GOTHIC STYLE–The style or architecture that began with Abbot Suger's reconstruction of the Abbey Church of St.-Denis, about 1140. It is the first style to incorporate the pointed arch and stained-glass windows, and the first to combine many arts and crafts into a single coordinated expression.

GROTESQUE–A fanciful carving, usually bizarre or ugly, whose function is to channel rainwater away from the walls by spraying it off the tip of a nose or tongue or the top of a head.

HARDPAN–A layer of firm compacted clay, considered a solid foundation material for building.

INFILL–Stones used to pave the area between ribs of an arch.

KEYSTONE–The wedge-shaped stone at the summit of an arch. Its weight and positioning locks the assembled stones in place.

LANCET–A narrow, pointed, arch-shaped opening, usually a window.

LECTERN–A reading desk, usually used for sermons.

LEWIS PIN–An ancient device for lifting stone. It consists of a dovetailed iron pin or tenon which fits into a mortice in the stone to be raised. A rope, called a "choker," is wrapped around the pins and pulled taut; pressure binds the pins against the stone which can then be safely lifted by a cable attached to the pins.

LIMESTONE–Calcium carbonate rock formed from the calcareous remains of organisms on the ocean floor.

MORTAR–The cementlike material used to bind stone together.

NAVE–The main chamber of a cathedral, stretching from the west end to the crossing.

PAD–The loading platform where masons prepare a stone to be raised to the level where it will be set.

PINNACLE–A tall, narrow, tapered structure that terminates a buttress, tower, turret, pier, etc.

PLUMB–To make vertical or to measure a vertical by using as a gauge a free-hanging cord drawn taut with a lead or steel weight–called a "plumb bob."

POINTING MORTAR–The fine-grained mortar used to fill masonry joints as a final precaution against moisture seeping between stones.

PORTAL–A main entranceway to a cathedral.

REREDOS–A decorated screen or section wall, usually carved wood or stone, behind an altar.

RIB–A single section of archwork spanning from a column cap to the keystone.

ROMANESQUE–The European architectural predecessor to Gothic characterized by a massive appearance and rounded archwork, modeled after the styles of ancient Rome.

ROSE WINDOW–A large round window above a portal with tracery that appears to radiate like rose petals from its center.

SEDILIA–Three seats in the chancel near the altar, reserved for clergy.

SLYPE–The passageway between the north transept and the administration building.

TEMPLET–A wooden pattern used by stone cutters as a guide for shaping blocks of stone to an architect's specifications.

TRANSEPT–The section of a cathedral that joins the nave at right angles at the crossing.

TRIFORIUM–An upper level of the nave inner aisles, sometimes used as a gallery.

TURRET–A small tower constructed at a corner of the main structure, often beginning several levels above the ground.

TYMPANUM–The space above a doorway, by the doorframe and the doorway arch. Tympanums are often filled with carving.

WROUGHT IRON–A purified form of iron specially prepared so that it is fibrous, tough, and malleable. Wrought iron contains less than 0.3 percent carbon and has been mechanically mixed with 1 or 2 percent slag so that it can be heated and quickly cooled without becoming brittle. Unlike cast iron, it is not shaped by pouring into a mold, but by being "wrought" or beaten into shape with special hammers and other tools.

(Photo by Hal Siegel)